The Holy Rosary through the
Visions of Saint Bridget of Sweden

The

Holy Rosary

Through the Visions of Saint Bridget of Sweden

FR. MARK HIGGINS

CATHOLIC WAY
PUBLISHING

Published in 2021 by Catholic Way Publishing.

Cover & Book design by Catholic Way Publishing.

Compiled and edited by Fr. Mark Higgins. Based on the book "Revelations of St. Bridget, on the life and passion of Our Lord, and the life of His Blessed Mother". Illustrations used in this book are works in the public domain.

This work is published for the greater glory of Jesus Christ through His most holy mother Mary and for the sanctification of the Church militant.

Ordering Information:

Orders by trade bookstores and wholesalers.

Please contact Ingram Content at www.ingramcontent.com.

ISBN-13: 978-1-78379-517-8 (PAPERBACK)

ISBN-13: 978-1-78379-518-5 (KINDLE E-BOOK)

ISBN-13: 978-1-78379-519-2 (EPUB E-BOOK)

10 9 8 7 6 5 4 3 2 1

Available in E-Book.

www.catholicwaypublishing.com

London, England, UK

2021

"Behold the handmaid of the Lord, be it done to me according to your word."

—THE BLESSED VIRGIN MARY, THE ANNUNCIATION

Contents

The Sorrowful Mysteries

35

The Glorious Mysteries

71

The Mysteries of Light

The Hopeful Mysteries

Introduction

S T. BRIDGET, WHILST STILL in her girlhood, in about her tenth year, was seized in ecstasy with a vision of her Blessed Saviour hanging upon the wood of the cross. This was the first of thousands of visions and dialogues between our saint and the heavenly court. In this first apparition the young girl tenderly asked Our Lord who had caused Him to suffer thus, to which He replied, "They who despise me, and spurn my love for them." St. Bridget would spend her entire life attempting to requite that love; to make up for the offences, sacrileges and indifference with which Our Lord has been so offended.

Bridget was born at the very beginning of one of the most painful centuries of Christendom, the Fourteenth, in the year of Our Lord 1303. The previous century had been blessed with some of the greatest saints of the Christian Era; the founding of the mendicant orders, great theologians, holy kings, and a venerable Pope, Innocent III, who had purged the church from evil, and called the clergy to a new degree of holiness and ascetic discipline. The Fourteenth would be a century of plague, famine, schism, failed crusades, fallen popes, anti-popes, the exile of the papacy to Avignon and the rise of the proto-protestants, in the form of Wycliffe and

Hus. This blessed woman, along with her contemporary, St. Catherine of Sienna, stood as a sign of contradiction and holiness amidst the century's sin, chastisements and infidelities. Blessed Bridget incessantly called for the conversion of the clergy, the return of the Holy Father to Rome; and for the laity, as much as the religious, to fall in homage before their Blessed Saviour and to rediscover Him, both as physically present in the Blessed Sacrament, and invisibly in their hearts through sanctifying grace.

Our Lady can be described as St. Bridget's personal novice mistress, it was under her guiding hand and inspiration that our holy saint was directed, both in temporal matters but, most profoundly, in the spiritual life, where the Blessed Mother instructed her for her greater sanctification. The Holy Virgin, with great familiarity, personally recounted to St. Bridget so many aspects of her life, and especially of her participation in her son's most dolorous passion; holy secrets, shared to a devout woman in the midst of a century in which love for God had grown cold, especially among the highest ranks of the clergy.

St. Bridget was compelled, through obligations and circumstances arising from her noble rank, to take marriage at a young age, and there, in that natural vocation she was blessed with the fruit of eight children and the companionship of a pious husband. In the environment of a truly Catholic home which she and her husband formed, she taught her children the truths of the faith, and instructed them as Our Lady had instructed her; guiding them in daily devotions, in the practice of penance and in the worthy reception of the sacraments. As God had blessed her, in His providence, with material prosperity, she and her husband shared generously with the poor and undertook many pilgrimages to the Holy Sanctuaries of Christendom. It was, indeed, upon returning from a family pilgrimage to Santiago de Compostela that her beloved husband passed away while still at a young age. St. Bridget, then a widow at only thirty years of age, realised a deeper supernatural call whispered into her ear by the saviour; not to take a new earthly husband, but to become a bride of Christ, and indeed, to found a new cloistered religious order for the relief of the sick and works of charity. She was willingly joined by her second daughter Catherine who became an enclosed member of the same order, taking up the evangelical councils, whilst the remainder, who had achieved majority according to the standards of the day, were either married or pursuing other religious vocations. The Catholic faith remained strong in her family, and until the evil days of the Swedish Reformation many of her descendants lead the religious houses of Sweden and continued her project of ascetic reform and the correction of abuses.

As a religious, St. Bridget necessarily travelled to Rome, to the See of Peter, in order to gain the necessary canonical approval for the statutes of her order, the Order of the Most Holy Saviour. Shocked by the evils and depravity of that city, which had once been empurpled by the blood of the holy martyrs, St. Bridget remained, a beacon of holiness and vocal opponent of vice, winning over wayward souls and constantly imploring the Holy Father to return to Rome from his evil exile in Avignon. After eventually heeding to her demands, and to the grace of Almighty God, the Holy Father returned and approved the statues of her congregation, which would later become known as the Birgittines. Never returning to her native land, and yet continually guiding from afar the fledgling monastic communities that embraced her rule, St. Bridget took flight from this world in the year of Our Lord 1373.

Bridget's life mission and vocation was fuelled by the constant revelations she received from the Heavenly Court, and in an age of great spiritual crisis she was strengthened both to guide her family in the ways of holiness and also to call the entire Church Militant to a true submission to its Divine head and founder.

In this book, for the first time, the revelations, which our saint received in the intimacies of prayer, are tied to the format of the Holy Rosary, so that, whilst united with St. Bridget in her efforts of spiritual revival and reform we may likewise be strengthened by the consolations of the same sacred visions. This era, in which God's providence has placed us, is undoubtedly no less dark than the age of our saint, with many of the same diabolical foes persecuting the true church from both within and without. Together, with her, we kneel before the Blessed Mother, in the very same spirit, in order to gain the spiritual nourishment so that, by a miracle, we might survive the great spiritual famine of our century, that our families might be sanctified, and that our own souls might be saved.

The visions of St. Bridget will both instruct and edify you, filling in many of the silences of Public Revelation and providing details for a richer meditation of the Holy Rosary. Allow yourself to take time and dwell upon the scenes St. Bridget will bring before your eyes, and receive with humble docility aspects of these sacred mysteries which, up till now, have remained unknown to you. It will be of no surprise to you that these writings, both in essence and in detail, show a remarkable harmony with the revelations of Blessed Anne Catherine Emmerich, which have been outlined in a previous work of rosary meditations. This book will act as a beautiful companion to that former work, but it also stands very much on its own, as St. Bridget received Our Lord and Our Lady's messages in her own unique manner, according to the natural dispositions in which God Himself formed her.

This work is offered in honour of religious sisters, called to be true spouses of Christ, called to an intimacy that, alas, so many have spurned and rejected in their love of things of this world and of a secular mentality. May our collective prayers convict and convert the female religious who have abandoned their ancient customs and forsaken the spirit and zeal of their founders. May the prayers of blessed Bridget inflame their souls with a spousal love for their divine Lord, in submission to Whom they are veiled. If the religious will not live as spouses, may the devotion of female laity make reparation for this infidelity, such that their devotion, and especially that of widows, may somehow requite the heart of Our Afflicted Saviour and bring down grace and mercy upon our world.

St. Bridget is widely known for the 'Fifteen Prayers of St. Bridget', which she received from Our Lord in honour of the number of His holy wounds endured during His sacred passion, 5480. These daily prayers, to be said for an entire year so as to equate the number of Our Lord's wounds, were of great popularity in Our Lady's Dowry of England on the eve of the evil Reformation. It is surely to be prayed that these prayers themselves may become better known and circulated, according to the graces which Our Lord will surely grant in accordance with their recitation. These prayers are included in the appendix at the end of this work. Whilst it must be acknowledge that in 1954 the Holy Office expressed a *dubium* over the exact nature of the promises attached to the daily practice of this devotion, the prayers themselves have been so widely endorsed, and by so many countless *beati,* that the certainty of receiving signal and extraordinary graces from them can hardly be doubted.

Yours, in the Immaculate Heart of Mary, Refuge of Sinners,
FR MARK HIGGINS

The Third Sunday of Lent, 2021
FRMARKHIGGINS@GMAIL.COM

NOTE ON PRAYING THE ROSARY USING THIS BOOK

If you are praying the rosary alone, it is suggested that you read the initial text before commencing the Our Father, afterwards the ten paragraphs of additional meditation could either be read before or during each Hail Mary. In a group setting a leader is required to read aloud each paragraph and commence each Hail Mary. The experience of the editor is that, in private use, with a prayerful silent reading of each passage, to say five mysteries will take at least 30 minutes and for some people closer to 45. If you feel the movements of grace pulling you into a simpler contemplation of a mystery as you read a paragraph, do not resist the Holy Spirit, and allow yourself to be at rest in the affect (the response of the heart) which Almighty God is stirring from within your soul.

In addition to the Fifteen Mysteries of the Holy Rosary,

meditations are also included for those who wish to consider the mysteries proposed by Pope John Paul II, the Mysteries of Light, and, additionally a further set of mysteries prepared by the author, the Hopeful Mysteries. These further mysteries allow the reader to contemplate additional material offered to us by our visionary and cover events prior to the Joyful Mysteries, these are given as — The Creation of all things in Christ, the Promise of the Redeemer and Co-Redemptrix, the Birth of the Immaculate Virgin Mary, the Presentation of Mary as a girl in the Temple, and the Chaste Espousals of Mary and Joseph.

It is customary to commence the Holy Rosary with the Sign of the Cross, the Apostles Creed, and then, for the intentions of the Holy Father, an Our Father, a Hail Mary, and a Glory Be. After completing five mysteries we then say some concluding prayers centred around the Hail Holy Queen, these are contained at the end of this short work.

The Joyful Mysteries

The Annunciation

THE FRUIT OF THIS MYSTERY

Humble adoration before Almighty God

HEN THE MOMENT ARRIVED, the moment when she knew that the Son of God would become her son, to take in her womb that human body which was to suffer as the prophets had foretold, who could measure her joy? Who could measure her sorrow? Like the rose, she had grown in beauty, but the thorns had grown too, stronger and sharper and more piercing. To Mary it was joy beyond words that her son should come in humility to lead man to heaven, saving him from the penalty which Adam's pride had incurred, the misery of hell. It was great sorrow that the sin of Adam by which man rebelled in both body and soul should require the redeeming death of her son in such agony of body and soul. It was great joy to her to conceive her son in sinlessness and purity. It was great sorrow to her that this so loved son was born to suffer a shameful death, and that she herself would be there to stand and see. The perfect rose blooms in beauty on its stem, and our delight is not spoiled by the sharp thorns around it. The sharp thorns of Mary's sorrow piercing her heart could not change her or weaken her will, and in her suffering she accepted whatever God's will should demand of her. We call her a Rose of Jericho, for men say that nowhere can so lovely a rose be found. In her holiness, Mary is more beautiful than all mankind, surpassed only by her son.

OUR FATHER   Our Father, Who art in Heaven, hallowed be Thy name, Thy kingdom come, Thy will be done, on earth as it is in heaven. Give us this day our daily bread; and forgive us our trespasses, as we forgive those who trespass against us; and lead us not into temptation, but deliver us from evil. Amen.

HAIL MARY (10)   Hail Mary, Full of Grace, the Lord is with thee. Blessed art thou among women and blessed is the fruit of thy womb, Jesus. Holy Mary, Mother of God, pray for us sinners now, and at the hour of our death. Amen.

1. Our Lord said, "Your ears were as pure and open as the most beautiful windows when Gabriel laid My will before you and

when I, God, became flesh in you. Your cheeks were of the fairest hue, white and red, for the fame of your praiseworthy deeds and the beauty of your character, which burned within you each day, were pleasing to Me. Truly, God My father rejoiced in the beauty of your character and never took His eyes away from you. By your love, all have obtained love. Your mouth was like a lamp, inwardly burning and outwardly shedding light, for the words and affections of your soul were inwardly on fire with divine understanding and shone outwardly in the graceful carriage of your body and the lovely harmony of your virtues. Truly, most dear mother, the word of your mouth somehow drew My divinity to you, and the fervour of your divine sweetness never separated Me from you, since your words were sweeter than honey and honeycomb"

2. Our Lady said, "Alone by myself and placing all my hope in God, an inspiration about God's great power came over me, and I recalled how the angels and everything created serve Him, and how His glory is indescribable and unlimited. While I was fascinated by this thought, I saw three wonderful things: I saw a star, but not the kind that shines in the sky; I saw a light, but not the kind that shines in this world; I smelled a fragrance, but not of herbs or anything else of this world. It was most delightful and truly indescribable, and it filled me up so completely that I was overcome with joy!"

3. "After this, I immediately heard a voice, but not from a human mouth, and when I heard it, I shuddered with great fear that it might be an illusion, or a mockery by an evil spirit. But shortly after this, an angel of God appeared before me; he was like the most handsome of men, but not in the flesh

as is the body of a created man, and he said to me, 'Hail, full of grace, the Lord is with thee!' When I heard this, I wondered what he meant and why he had come to me with such a greeting, for I knew and believed that I was unworthy of any such thing, or any good thing! However, I also knew that nothing is impossible for God, if He desires it."

4. "Then the angel spoke to me again, 'The child to be born in you is holy and will be called the Son of God. May His will be done as it pleases Him.' But, not even then did I consider myself worthy, and I did not ask the angel why, or when, this would happen. Instead I asked him how it could be that I, an unworthy maiden, who did not know any man, should become the Mother of God. The angel answered me (as I have just said), 'Nothing is impossible for God, for whatever He wants to do will be done.'"

5. "When I had heard these words of the angel, I felt the most fervent desire to become the Mother of God, and my soul spoke out of love and desire, saying, 'See, here I am; your will be done in me!' With these words, my son was conceived in my womb to the indescribable joy of my soul and my every limb! While I had Him in my womb, I carried Him without any pain, without any heaviness or discomfort. I humbled myself in all things, knowing that He Whom I bore was the Almighty!"

6. The Lord Jesus said to Mary, "Blessed are you, My most beloved Mother! My angel Gabriel said to you, "Blessed are you, Mary, among women!" And I bear witness to you that you are blessed and most holy above all the choirs of angels.

You are like a flower in a garden that is surrounded by other fragrant flowers, but surpasses them all in scent, beauty, and virtue. These flowers are all the chosen men from Adam to the end of the world which were planted in the garden of the world and shone and smelled in manifold virtues. But among all of those who were and who will afterward come, you were the greatest in the fragrance of humility and a good life, in the beauty of the most pleasing virginity, and in the virtue of abstinence. For I bear witness to you that you were more than any martyr at the time of My suffering, more than any confessor in your abstinence, and more than any angel in your mercy and good will."

7. "The Divinity sent its Word to the Virgin Mary through the angel Gabriel. After the angel had delivered his message, the Word was made flesh in the Virgin. I, Who speak with you, am that Word. The Father sent Me by the Holy Spirit into the womb of the Virgin, although not in such a way that the angels would be left without the vision and presence of God. Rather, I, the Son, Who was with the Father and the Holy Spirit in the virginal womb, remained the same God in the sight of the angels in heaven together with the Father and the Spirit, ruling and sustaining all things."

8. All who hold the true faith must rejoice unceasingly at this union achieved through Mary. The Son of God took in her womb true flesh and blood, and true humanity, not losing His divinity: in divinity was humanity, in humanity divinity. Christ did not lose His divinity, nor Mary her virginity. True God, He came as man to men, withholding from the eyes of men His divinity seen ever by the angels in heaven.

9. Picture some king, honoured by all, with great power and possessions, and someone dear to him suffering great insult and injury; if the king took on himself the burden of his friend, if he gave all his wealth to save him from poverty, still more, if he offered his life for his friend, would not this be the greatest love he could show? But no love of men on earth could equal the love of God in heaven. No love could equal that love which led God to condescend to our need, and entrust Himself to the womb of the Virgin Mary and take there our humanity.

10. Mary is like that bush which Moses saw, burning yet never consumed by the fire. God Himself was there, and He made known His name to Moses — I am Who am, the name of the eternal. To God, to the Angels, to Adam, to the Patriarchs and the Prophets, and to countless servants of God, this Burning Bush, which was Mary, brought joy beyond words. Mary, in the fire of her love, conceived the Son of God. Mary is the gateway by which Christ entered into this world, to open to man the gate of heaven. Pray then, pray then to Mary, that at death she may come to us, to secure for us entry into the eternal kingdom of Christ, her son.

GLORY BE TO THE FATHER   Glory be to the Father, and to the Son, and to the Holy Spirit, as it was in the beginning, is now and ever shall be, world without end. Amen.

THE FATIMA PRAYER   O my Jesus, forgive us our sins, save us from the fires of hell, lead all souls to heaven, especially those in most need of Thy mercy.

The Visitation

THE FRUIT OF THIS MYSTERY

Charity to one's neighbour

MARY SAID, "I STAND over the world in continuous prayer, like a rainbow above the clouds that appears to bend towards the earth and to touch it with both ends. I see myself as a rainbow bending down towards both the good and the wicked by means of my prayers. I bend down toward good people in order that they may be steadfast in the commandments of the holy church, and I bend down toward bad people in order that they may not add to their wickedness and grow worse."

OUR FATHER   Our Father, Who art in Heaven, hallowed be Thy name, Thy kingdom come, Thy will be done, on earth as it is in heaven. Give us this day our daily bread; and forgive us our trespasses, as we forgive those who trespass against us; and lead us not into temptation, but deliver us from evil. Amen.

HAIL MARY (10)   Hail Mary, Full of Grace, the Lord is with thee. Blessed art thou among women and blessed is the fruit of thy womb, Jesus. Holy Mary, Mother of God, pray for us sinners now, and at the hour of our death. Amen.

1. The Eternal Word spoke, "I am the Creator of the heavens and the earth, one in divinity with the Father and the Holy Spirit. I am the One Who spoke to the patriarchs and the prophets and the One Whom they awaited. For the sake of their longing and in agreement with My promise, I assumed flesh without sin and concupiscence, by entering the womb of the Virgin like the sun shining through the clearest gem. For just as the sun does not damage the glass by entering it, likewise the virginity of the Virgin was not lost when I assumed manhood. I assumed flesh in such a way that I did not have to forsake My divinity, and I was no less God, with the Father and the Holy Spirit, governing and upholding all things, although I was in the womb of the Virgin in My human nature. Just as brightness is never separated from fire, so too, My divinity was never separated from My humanity, not even in death."

2. The Word spoke to the Virgin, "Your womb, O daughter, was as pure as ivory and was like a space made out of gems of virtue, for you never grew lukewarm and could not be damaged by tribulation. The walls of your womb, that is, of your faith, were like gleaming gold, and on them the strength of your virtues was recorded, your prudence and justice and temperance along with perfect perseverance, for all your virtues were perfected with divine charity. Your womb was a spiritual and physical space so desirable to Me and your soul was so pleasing to Me that I did not disdain to come down to you from the highest heaven and to dwell in you. No, rather, I was most pleased and delighted."

3. Almighty God spoke to the saint, "O bride of Christ, St. Bridget, I assure you that just as Zechariah and Elizabeth rejoiced in their souls with an unspeakable joy over the promise of a future child, you too, shall rejoice over My grace that I want to give you, and thereby, which others will rejoice through you. An angel spoke to Zechariah and Elizabeth, but I, the God and Creator of the angels, want to speak to you. Elizabeth gave birth to My most dear friend John, but I want many sons to be born to Me through you, O bride of Christ, not of the flesh but of the spirit."

4. The Son explained, "As to why I lay so long in the womb of the Virgin, I answer, I am the founder of all nature and have arranged for each and every nature a due measure and time and order of birth. If I, the founder of nature, had emerged from the womb as soon as I had been conceived, then I would have acted against the natural arrangement, and My taking on a human nature would have then been fantastic

and unreal. Therefore, I wished to remain in the womb as long as other children, so that I, too, might fulfil My own wise arrangements of the natural order in My own case. My limbs grew over intervals of time, although I was as full of wisdom at the start of My birth as at the end."

5. John the Baptist said, "Blessed are You, O God! You pre-exist all things. There has never been another god together with You or besides You nor will there ever be any after You. You are the truth promised by the prophets. While yet unborn I rejoiced in You. I recognised You more fully when I pointed You out. You are our joy and our glory, our longing and our delight. The sight of You fills us with an indescribable pleasure, which no one knows but the one who has tasted of it. You are our only love. It is no wonder that we love You, for You are love itself, and You love not only those who love You but, being the creator of all, You are even charitable to those who scorn You."

6. When John the Baptist was born, it caused such displeasure to the devils that it was as though a voice resounded from hell saying, "A miraculous child has been born. What shall we do? If we attack him with pride, he scorns to listen to us and much less wants to obey our suggestion. If we offer him riches, he turns his back on us and refuses to look, and if we offer him sensual pleasure, he is like a dead man and cannot feel it."

7. "In truth, I tell you, John was like a flower full of sweetness and honey, for never did anything unclean or superfluous enter his mouth, and he never received the necessities of

life over the limits of what he needed. He lived in complete opposition to all thoughts and deeds of impurity, for this reason he can rightly be called an angel and a virgin for the divine life that he lived."

8. As we read about in the life of blessed John the Baptist, we realise that many times the merits of parents cooperate to produce in their children an even greater grace, a grace which perseveres to the end.

9. The Son of God said, "In this beehive, that is, in the Holy Church, there are two kinds of people, just as there are two kinds of bees. The first ones are those bad Christians who do not gather nectar for Me but for themselves. They return carrying nothing back and do not recognise their leader. They have a sting instead of honey and lust instead of love. The good bees represent good Christians. They show Me respect in three ways. First, they hold Me as their leader and Lord, offering Me sweet honey, that is, works of charity, which are pleasing to Me and useful to themselves. Second, they wait upon My will; their will accords with My will, all their thought is on My passion, all their actions are for My glory. Third, they follow Me, that is, they obey Me in everything."

10. The Virgin said, "After I gave my consent to the messenger of God, Joseph, seeing my womb swell by virtue of the Holy Spirit, feared very greatly. Not suspecting me of anything sinister, but mindful of the sayings of the prophets who had foretold that the Son of God would be born of a virgin, he reckoned himself unworthy to serve such a mother until the

angel instructed him in his sleep not to be afraid but to serve me with charity."

GLORY BE TO THE FATHER   Glory be to the Father, and to the Son, and to the Holy Spirit, as it was in the beginning, is now and ever shall be, world without end. Amen.

THE FATIMA PRAYER   O my Jesus, forgive us our sins, save us from the fires of hell, lead all souls to heaven, especially those in most need of Thy mercy.

The Nativity of Jesus Christ

HE MOTHER OF GOD spoke, "There is the same humility in my son now in the power of His Godhead as there was when He was laid in the manger. Although He knew all things in accordance with His Godhead, nevertheless, while lying between two animals, He spoke nothing at all, in accordance with His humanity. So too now, sitting at the right hand of the Father, He hears all who speak to Him with love; and He answers through infusions of the Holy Spirit. To some He speaks with words and thoughts, to others as if from mouth to mouth, just as it pleases Him."

OUR FATHER   Our Father, Who art in Heaven, hallowed be Thy name, Thy kingdom come, Thy will be done, on earth as it is in heaven. Give us this day our daily bread; and forgive us our trespasses, as we forgive those who trespass against us; and lead us not into temptation, but deliver us from evil. Amen.

HAIL MARY (10)   Hail Mary, Full of Grace, the Lord is with thee. Blessed art thou among women and blessed is the fruit of thy womb, Jesus. Holy Mary, Mother of God, pray for us sinners now, and at the hour of our death. Amen.

1. Mary said, "Joseph and I reserved nothing for ourselves except the necessities of life, the rest we let go, for the love of God. When my son's hour of birth was at hand, an hour that I very well knew beforehand, I came, in accord with God's foreknowledge, to Bethlehem, bringing with me, for my son, clean clothing and cloths that no one had ever used before. In them I wrapped, for the first time, Him Who was born from me in all purity. And even though from eternity it was foreseen that I would sit in honour on a most sublime seat above all creatures and above all human beings, yet nonetheless, in my humility, I did not disdain to prepare and serve the things that were necessary for myself and Joseph."

2. St. Bridget revealed, "When I was at the manger of the Lord in Bethlehem, I saw a Virgin, pregnant and very beautiful, clothed in a white mantle and a finely woven tunic. Her

womb was full and much swollen, for she was now ready to give birth. With her there was a very dignified old man; and with them they had both an ox and an ass. When they had entered the cave, and after the ox and the ass had been tied to the manger, the old man went outside and brought to the Virgin a lighted candle and fixed it in the wall and went outside in order not to be personally present at the birth."

3. "And so the Virgin then took the shoes from her feet, put off the white mantle that covered her, removed the veil from her head, and laid these things beside her, remaining in only her tunic, with her most beautiful hair, as if of gold, spread out upon her shoulder blades. She then drew out two small cloths of linen and two of wool, very clean and finely woven, which she carried with her to wrap the infant that was to be born, and two other small linens to cover and bind His head; and she laid these cloths beside her that she might use them in due time."

4. "And when all these things had thus been prepared, then the Virgin knelt with great reverence, putting herself at prayer; and she kept her back toward the manger and her face lifted to heaven toward the east. And so, with raised hands and with her eyes intent on heaven, she was as if suspended in an ecstasy of contemplation, inebriated with divine sweetness. And while she was praying, I saw the One lying in her womb then move; and then and there, in a moment and the twinkling of an eye, she gave birth to a son, from Whom there went out such great and ineffable light and splendour that the sun could not be compared to it. Nor did that candle that the old man had put in place give light at all because that

divine splendour totally annihilated the material splendour of the candle."

5. "And so sudden and momentary was that manner of giving birth that I was unable to notice or discern how or in what member she was giving birth. But yet, at once, I saw that glorious infant lying on the earth, naked and glowing in the greatest of neatness. His flesh was most clean of all filth and uncleanness. I saw also the afterbirth, lying wrapped, neatly beside him. And then I heard the wonderfully sweet and most dulcet songs of the angels. And the Virgin's womb, which before the birth had been very swollen, at once retracted; and her body then looked wonderfully beautiful and delicate."

6. "When therefore the Virgin felt that she had now given birth, at once, having bowed her head and joined her hands, with great dignity and reverence she adored the boy and said to Him, 'Welcome, my God, my Lord, and my son!' And then the boy, crying and, as it were, trembling from the cold and the hardness of the pavement where He lay, rolled a little and extended His limbs, seeking to find refreshment and His Mother's favour. Then his Mother took Him in her hands and pressed Him to her breast, and with cheek and breast she warmed him with great joy and tender maternal compassion. Then, sitting on the earth, she put her son in her lap and cut His umbilical cord with her fingers. At once it was cut off, and from it no liquid or blood went out. Then she began to wrap Him carefully, first in the linen cloths and then in the woollen, binding His little body, legs, and arms with a ribbon that had been sewn into four parts of the outer woollen cloth.

And afterward she wrapped and tied on the boy's head those two small linen cloths that she had prepared for this purpose."

7. Mary said, "When I gave birth to Him, it was also without any pain or sin, just as I had conceived Him, but with such exaltation and joy of soul and body that my feet did not feel the ground where they had been standing because of this indescribable joy! Just as He had entered my limbs to the joy of all my soul, He left my body, leaving my virginity intact, and my soul and whole body in a state of indescribable joy and jubilation. When I gazed upon and contemplated His beauty, joy seeped through my soul like dewdrops and I knew myself to be unworthy of such a son. But when I considered the places where nails would be pierced through His hands and feet at the crucifixion, my eyes filled with tears and my heart was almost torn apart by sorrow"

8. St. Bridget said, "When these things were accomplished, the old man, St Joseph, entered, and prostrating on the earth, he adored the child on bended knee and wept for joy. Not even at the birth was that Virgin changed in colour or by infirmity. Nor did she experience the same bodily weakness that comes for women after giving birth. Our Lady therefore arose, and, holding the boy in her arms, put Him in the manger. Then both of them, on their bended knees, continued to adore the child with gladness and immense joy."

9. Our Lady said, "My daughter, know that when the three Magi kings came into the stable to adore my son, I had foreknown their coming well in advance. And when they entered and adored Him, then my son exulted, and for joy

He had then a more cheerful face. I too rejoiced exceedingly, and, while being attentive to their words and actions, kept those things in my mind and reflected on them in my heart."

10. Our Lord said, "My flight into Egypt revealed the frailty of My human nature and fulfilled a prophecy. I also set an example for those to come, because persecution should at times be avoided for God's greater glory. My escape from My pursuers showed that My divine plan surpassed human plans, for it is not easy to fight against God. Furthermore, the slaying of the infants was a sign of My future passion, and a mystery of vocation and divine charity. Although the infants themselves did not bear witness to Me with their voices and mouths, they bore witness by their deaths, as befitted My own infancy. Indeed it had been foreseen that the praise of God would be fulfilled even by the blood of innocents. And although the malice of the unjust fell upon them, My divine permission allowed it to disclose human malice and My own incomprehensible purpose. Indeed, when Herod's foul anger erupted against the boys there merit and grace justly abounded, and although there was no verbal testimony or proper age, their bloodshed brought them the highest good."

GLORY BE TO THE FATHER   Glory be to the Father, and to the Son, and to the Holy Spirit, as it was in the beginning, is now and ever shall be, world without end. Amen.

THE FATIMA PRAYER   O my Jesus, forgive us our sins, save us from the fires of hell, lead all souls to heaven, especially those in most need of Thy mercy.

The Presentation in the Temple

THE FRUIT OF THIS MYSTERY

The grace of a happy death

 MOTHER'S JOY IS COMPLETE when her child is born and she sees it healthy and perfectly formed. Her pain and anxiety are over. Mary rejoiced at Christ's birth, but she knew that no moment of her life would be free of sorrow. The prophets foretold, long before the coming of Christ, His sufferings and death. Simeon foretold, in the presence of Mary and her child, the piercing of her heart by a sword of sorrow. We know that the mind is more sensitive to pain even than the body. We know that the soul of Mary, even before the death of her son, would feel that sword of sorrow more sharply than all women on earth would feel the suffering of childbearing. Each day brought nearer the sufferings of Christ. Each day brought nearer the piercing of Mary's heart. It was the compassion of Christ alone which enabled her, by His presence and His words, to bear day by day such piercing sorrow.

OUR FATHER   Our Father, Who art in Heaven, hallowed be Thy name, Thy kingdom come, Thy will be done, on earth as it is in heaven. Give us this day our daily bread; and forgive us our trespasses, as we forgive those who trespass against us; and lead us not into temptation, but deliver us from evil. Amen.

HAIL MARY (10)   Hail Mary, Full of Grace, the Lord is with thee. Blessed art thou among women and blessed is the fruit of thy womb, Jesus. Holy Mary, Mother of God, pray for us sinners now, and at the hour of our death. Amen.

1. While Lady Bridget, the bride of Christ, was in Rome, in the church called Saint Mary Major, on the feast of the Purification of the Blessed Virgin Mary, she was caught up into a spiritual vision, and saw that in heaven, as it were, all things were being prepared for a great feast. And then she saw, as it were, a temple of wondrous beauty; and there too was that venerable and just old man, Simeon, ready to receive the child Jesus in his arms with supreme longing and gladness. She also saw the Blessed Virgin most honourably

enter, carrying her young son to offer Him in the temple according to the law of the Lord.

2. And then she saw a countless multitude of angels and of the various ranks of the saintly men of God and of His saintly virgins and ladies, all going before the Blessed Virgin-Mother of God and surrounding her with all joy and devotion. Before her an angel carried a long, very broad, and bloody sword which signified those very great sorrows which Mary suffered at the death of her most loving son and which were prefigured by that sword which the just man Simeon prophesied would pierce her soul. And while all the heavenly court exulted, this was said to the bride, "See with what great honour and glory the Queen of Heaven is, on this feast, recompensed for the sword of sorrows which she endured at the passion of her beloved son."

3. At the moment of Christ's birth, as Our Lady held Him for the first time in her arms, she foresaw the fulfilment of prophecy. As she wrapped Him in swaddling-clothes, she foresaw the scourging of His flesh which would make Him a leper in the eyes of men. The hands and feet of her child brought the thought of the nails which would pierce them. The face of her son, beautiful beyond the beauty of men, was the face men would spit on. His cheeks would feel the blows of their hatred. His ears would hear the curses of their defiance. No part of that sacred body would escape the bitterness of that most bitter death. And when all breathing ceased, there would still be the soldier's sharp spear to pierce His lifeless heart.

4. If the prophets foresaw these things, would not Mary foresee them, even more clearly? She was the mother predestined for the Son of God. How could she not have foreseen His sufferings when He took flesh in her womb for this very purpose? The presence of the Holy Spirit would enlighten her, so that she knew better than the Prophets that things which they, through the Holy Spirit, had foretold.

5. St. Bridget said, in words that apply to the just old man Simeon, "When this friend of mine came to the end of his life and his soul left his body, five legions of angels were sent to greet him. Along with them there also came a multitude of demons in order to find out if they could lay any claim to him, for they are full of malice and never rest from malice. A bright clear voice was then heard in heaven, the voice of the Son, saying, 'My Lord and Father, is not this the man who bound himself to Your will and carried it out to perfection?' The man himself then answered in his own conscience, 'Indeed I am.' To which the Almighty replied, 'You are My servant and you have done My will. Come to Me, your Almighty Creator and dear Father! An eternal inheritance is owed to you, for you are a son. Your Father's inheritance is owed to you, for you have been obedient.'"

6. "This man meditated on God in his heart at all times. He had Him on his lips, in his works, and yearned for Him above all things. Out of his love and veneration he caused himself to die to the world. In return for a little struggle, this man has deserved eternal rest and joy with his God for Whom he yearned so much and so often!"

7. The separation of body and soul is for the righteous no more than a dream, for they wake up to life eternal. That which should be called death is when the soul separates from the body in an eternal death.

8. The Lord said, "There are many people who, while not mindful of the life to come, wish to die a Christian death. Now, what does a Christian death mean, if not to die as I died, innocently, willingly and patiently? Am I then contemptible because My death was contemptible and harsh? Or are My chosen ones foolish, because they had to bear contemptible sufferings? I and My chosen ones did indeed suffer harshly, but did so in order to show by word and example that the way to heaven is difficult, and in order to make people realise fully how necessary purification is for the wicked, seeing that the innocent elect suffered so greatly."

9. "Know, then, that a person dies a contemptible and evil death when he dies while living a dissolute life and with the intention of sinning, when he has worldly success and desires to live for a long time but does not remember to give thanks to God. The person who dies happily loves God with his whole heart, and even though he may be struck down by a despicable death or afflicted by a chronic illness, he knows that his harsh death lessens his sins, as well as the punishment for sin, and increases his reward."

10. The Lord said, referring to the passing of the just man, "His soul saw it all and said to itself in exultation, 'Happy am I to have been created! Happy am I to have served my God Whom I now behold! Happy am I, for I have joy and glory

that will never end!' In this way My friend came to Me and received his reward. Although not everyone sheds his blood for the sake of My name, nevertheless, everyone will receive the same reward, provided they have the intention of giving their lives for Me if the occasion presents itself and the needs of the faith demand it. See how important a good intention is!"

GLORY BE TO THE FATHER   Glory be to the Father, and to the Son, and to the Holy Spirit, as it was in the beginning, is now and ever shall be, world without end. Amen.

THE FATIMA PRAYER   O my Jesus, forgive us our sins, save us from the fires of hell, lead all souls to heaven, especially those in most need of Thy mercy.

The Finding of the Boy
Jesus in the Temple

THE FRUIT OF THIS MYSTERY

Submission of intellect and will to the holy doctrines of Christ

T HE MOTHER OF GOD spoke again, "Though you cannot see my son as He exists in heaven, hear at least of the appearance of His body when He was on earth. He was so fair of face that no one, not even someone very sad at heart, could see Him face-to-face without being cheered at His sight. The righteous were cheered with spiritual comfort, but even the wicked found relief from the sorrow of the world for as long as they looked on Him. For that reason, people who were sad used to say, 'Let us go and see Mary's son and at least find some relief as long as we are there.'"

OUR FATHER   Our Father, Who art in Heaven, hallowed be Thy name, Thy kingdom come, Thy will be done, on earth as it is in heaven. Give us this day our daily bread; and forgive us our trespasses, as we forgive those who trespass against us; and lead us not into temptation, but deliver us from evil. Amen.

HAIL MARY (10)   Hail Mary, Full of Grace, the Lord is with thee. Blessed art thou among women and blessed is the fruit of thy womb, Jesus. Holy Mary, Mother of God, pray for us sinners now, and at the hour of our death. Amen.

1. "You shall seek Me and shall not find Me." These words of Christ were the sharp point of the sword of sorrow, entering Mary's heart.

2. Mary said, "It is a terrible thing that the Lord of all things and the King of glory is despised. He was like a pilgrim on earth, wandering from place to place, knocking on many doors, like a wayfarer seeking welcome. When my son came dressed as a pilgrim to the first house, He knocked on the door and said, 'Friend, open up and let Me enter to rest and stay with you, so that the wild animals do not harm Me, so that storm-showers and rain may not fall upon Me! Give me some of your clothes to warm Me from the cold, to cover Me in My nakedness! Give me some of your food to refresh

Me in my hunger and something to drink to revive Me. You will receive a reward from your God!'"

3. Once, the Lord said to His mother, "I, Who lay in your womb and assumed Manhood from you, liken Myself with this staff of Moses. First, I am as terrifying to My enemies as the staff that transformed into a snake. For they flee from Me as from the sight of a snake, and they are terrified of Me and abhor Me like a venomous snake; and yet I am without the venom of malice and am instead all full of mercy. I allow Myself to be held by them, if they want. I return to them if they search for Me. If they call on Me I run to them like a mother to her lost and recovered son. If they cry out to Me I give them My mercy and forgive their sins. This is what I do for them, and yet they abhor Me like a venomous snake."

4. We read that the Queen of Sheba made the long journey from her own lands in the south to visit Solomon the King. Her journey was not wasted, for she found great delight in his words. No gifts were too precious for her to give, no praise too high, and she departed in admiration of such great wisdom. The Virgin Mary spent long hours in thought, considering the course of events in this world, and all the things that this world holds dear. Nothing delighted or attracted her, except the wisdom she had learned from God. This was her desire and her search, and she did not rest till she had found it in Christ. In the Son of God the Holy Virgin found wisdom infinitely greater than Solomon's. The Queen of Sheba was overcome with wonder as she contemplated the wisdom of Solomon. Mary was overcome with sorrow as she pondered the loving wisdom of Christ, Who saw salvation in suffering,

and willed to save man from subjection to Satan by His sufferings and cross.

5. Our Lady said, "My daughter, seek wisdom from the Wise One, I mean, from My son! He is wisdom itself from Whom all wisdom comes. He is the circle that never ends. I entreat you as a mother does her child, love this wisdom that is like gold on the inside but contemptible on the outside, it burns inside with love, but requires effort to obtain."

6. Our Lord said, "As to why I did not disclose My divinity to people in general, I answer, although the devil lost the dignity of his first state, still he did not lose his cunning, which belongs to him for the trial of the good and for his own shame. In order that My human form might grow and reach its determined age, it was necessary to hide the mystery of My divinity from the devil, because I wanted to enter hidden into combat with the devil, and because I resolved to be despised in order to overthrow human pride. The very teachers of the law despised Me because I came as a humble man, and, because they were proud, they did not want to hear about true justice, which comes from the faith in My redemption. They shall therefore be confounded when the 'son of perdition' comes in his pride. Will such proud men enter heaven? Certainly not! I came as a humble man in order that the people might learn humility. And I hid Myself from the proud, because they wished to understand neither My justice nor their very selves."

7. Mary said, "As my son Jesus Christ, true God and wisest of men, lay in my womb, I received such great wisdom

through Him that I not only could understand the learning of scholars, I could even discern whether their hearts were true, whether their words proceeded from love for God or from mere scholarly cleverness."

8. The Lord said, "My friends are like scholars who have wisdom without human aid, for I Myself teach them inwardly and they are full of the sweetness and divine love with which they defeat the devil. But nowadays people study in a different way. First, they want to be wise out of vainglory in order to be called good students and masterly scholars. Second, they want to be wise in order to own and win riches. Third, they want to be wise in order to win honours and privileges. That is why I left them when they went to their schools and entered there, since they studied because of pride, but I taught them humility. They enter the schools for the sake of greed, but I had no place to rest My head. They enter in order to win privileges, envying those more highly placed than themselves, but I was judged by Pilate and mocked by Herod. That is why I will leave them, because they are not learning My wisdom."

9. The Lord said, "Whoever, then, has the grace of greater understanding should beware of the danger of a harsher judgment if he or she is negligent. Whoever lacks understanding and intellectual brilliance should take advantage of the little he has and do what he can, for he has been saved from many occasions of sin. In youth even Peter the Apostle was forgetful, and John unlearned. Yet they grasped true wisdom in old age, for they sought the source of wisdom. Solomon was quick to learn when young, and Aristotle had a subtle mind. However, they did not grasp the origin of wisdom, for they

neither glorified the giver of wisdom, as they should have, nor put into practice what they knew and taught, nor studied in order to improve themselves but to improve others. It is not scholarship that is pleasing to Me but a good way of life. It is necessary to correct those who abuse their reasoning faculty, for I, the God and Lord of all, give knowledge to humankind, and I correct both wise and unwise."

10. The Almighty said, "The Mother of Mercy, shall introduce to My son everyone whom obedience nourishes in the lap of humility, everyone whom the faith feeds with the food of sweetness, everyone whom patience dresses in the arms of virtue, and My son will crown that person with His sweet crown."

GLORY BE TO THE FATHER   Glory be to the Father, and to the Son, and to the Holy Spirit, as it was in the beginning, is now and ever shall be, world without end. Amen.

THE FATIMA PRAYER   O my Jesus, forgive us our sins, save us from the fires of hell, lead all souls to heaven, especially those in most need of Thy mercy.

CONCLUDING PRAYERS   *Upon completing the recitation of the Holy Rosary, the following prayers are customary, but others too may be added according to one's devotion and preference.*

HAIL HOLY QUEEN   Hail Holy Queen, Mother of Mercy, hail our life, our sweetness and our hope. To thee do we cry, poor banished children of Eve, to thee do we send up our sighs, mourning and weeping in this vale of tears. Turn then, most gracious advocate, thine eyes of mercy towards us, and after this, our exile, show unto us the blessed fruit of thy womb, Jesus. O clement, O loving, O sweet Virgin Mary. Pray for us O holy Mother of God, that we may be made worthy of the promises of Christ.

Let Us Pray   O God, Whose only begotten son, by His life, death and resurrection, has purchased for us the rewards of eternal life, grant we beseech Thee, that meditating on these mysteries of the most Holy Rosary of the Blessed Virgin Mary, we may both imitate what they contain and obtain what they promise, through the same Christ our Lord. Amen.

PRAYER TO SAINT MICHAEL THE ARCHANGEL   Holy Michael, the Archangel, defend us in the day of battle. Be our safeguard against the wickedness and snares of the devil. May God rebuke him, we humbly pray; and do thou, O Prince of the heavenly hosts, by the power of God thrust down into hell Satan and all the evil spirits who wander through the world seeking the ruin of souls. Amen.

MEMORARE   Remember, O most gracious Virgin Mary, that never was it known that anyone who fled to thy protection, implored thy help, or sought thine intercession was left unaided. Inspired by this confidence, I fly unto thee, O Virgin of virgins, my mother; to thee do I come, before thee I stand, sinful and sorrowful. O Mother of the Word Incarnate, despise not my petitions, but in thy mercy hear and answer me. Amen.

May the Divine Assistance remain always with us, and may the souls of the faithful departed, through the mercy of God rest in peace. Amen.

The Sorrowful Mysteries

The Agony in the Garden

THE FRUIT OF THIS MYSTERY

The grace to endure persecution for Christ's sake

HO IS ABLE TO meditate worthily enough on the agony of Christ's human nature, the agony that He was undergoing at the moment when He prayed for the chalice of His passion to be taken from Him and when drops of His blood came from His body? That sweat was bloody indeed, because the blood of His human nature was consumed with the natural fear He was suffering in order to show that He was true man, not a pure spirit, immune to suffering.

OUR FATHER   Our Father, Who art in Heaven, hallowed be Thy name, Thy kingdom come, Thy will be done, on earth as it is in heaven. Give us this day our daily bread; and forgive us our trespasses, as we forgive those who trespass against us; and lead us not into temptation, but deliver us from evil. Amen.

HAIL MARY (10)   Hail Mary, Full of Grace, the Lord is with thee. Blessed art thou among women and blessed is the fruit of thy womb, Jesus. Holy Mary, Mother of God, pray for us sinners now, and at the hour of our death. Amen.

1. The Blessed Mother said, "At the time of my son's suffering, when His betrayer Judas approached, He bent down, for Judas was small of size, and gave him a kiss, and said, 'Friend, for what have you come?' And some of those there seized Him immediately, while others pulled Him by the hair or defiled Him with their spittle."

2. The Lord said, "Three good things were revealed in Me through the effrontery of Judas. First, My patience is to be praised because, though I knew who My betrayer was, I did not reject his company. Second, My power was revealed when, in the presence of My betrayer, all those who were with him fell to the ground at a single word of Mine. Third, the divine wisdom and love were manifested, since I transformed all the wickedness of Judas and the devil into salvation for souls."

3. My Lord Jesus Christ, You were sold by Your disciple and bought by the Jews, You were made a captive for our sake. Solely by Your word, You cast Your enemies to the earth; and then of Your own will You gave Yourself over as a captive to their unclean and grasping hands.

4. O Lord, remember the sadness and bitterness which You experienced in Your soul as You Yourself bore witness saying, "My soul is sorrowful even unto death." Remember the fear, anguish and pain that You suffered in Your delicate body, having prayed three times, bathed in a sweat of blood. You had been betrayed by Judas, Your disciple. You were then arrested by the people of the nation You had chosen and elevated. You were accused by false witnesses and unjustly judged by three judges during the flower of Your youth and during the Solemn Paschal Season. In memory of all these pains and sufferings which You endured before Your passion on the cross, grant me before my death, true contrition, a sincere and entire confession worthy satisfaction and the remission of all my sins.

5. The Lord said, "In order that My friends should not fear that they are abandoned when the moment of tribulation comes to them, I showed them in Myself that the weak flesh always flees from suffering. Justice did not allow My manhood to enter into glory without suffering, although I was able to do so by the power of My divinity."

6. The Blessed Mother spoke, "When my son's passion was near at hand, tears filled His eyes and sweat covered His body

from fear of suffering. Next, He was taken from my sight, and I did not see Him again until He was led out to be scourged."

7. "Just as Judas was shut out and cut off from the sacred number of the apostles by betraying Christ my son, in like manner, those who have rejected the Catholic faith are cut off and cast out from the number of the whole flock of Christianity in the just judgment of the Divine Majesty. Know that, even so, all those who want to amend their lives will obtain mercy from God."

8. The Lord said, "You wondered, My bride, why I am so patient with evil. That is because I am merciful and My justice and mercy endures and spares sinners for the present time. My justice endures them so that their time may be fully completed. It was in order to reveal God's glory and patience that I tolerated Pilate, Herod, and Judas, even though they were evil and damned. If anyone questions why I tolerate this or that person, let him regard Judas and Pilate."

9. The Holy Virgin said, "Pilate knew very well that my son had not sinned and did not deserve to die, but he, nonetheless, felt compelled to judge my son to death because he feared the loss of his worldly power and the revolt of the Jews. But what do the enemies of my son, who are in the world today, have to fear in serving Him? What honour or dignity will they lose by honouring Him? They will be judged with a more severe sentence than Pilate's, for they are worse than him in my son's sight."

10. The sword of sorrow pierced deeper into Our Lady's soul at the betrayal of Judas, and at the arrest of Christ, when He willed to be taken by the enemies of justice and truth. Deeper still the sword pierced at each insult offered to Christ, with each suffering inflicted on Him. The sorrow of her heart overflowed into all the members of her body. She saw how cruelly Christ was struck, and more cruelly beaten and scourged. She heard the calls of death by the Jews and the cries of the people.

GLORY BE TO THE FATHER   Glory be to the Father, and to the Son, and to the Holy Spirit, as it was in the beginning, is now and ever shall be, world without end. Amen.

THE FATIMA PRAYER   O my Jesus, forgive us our sins, save us from the fires of hell, lead all souls to heaven, especially those in most need of Thy mercy.

The Scourging at the Pillar

THE FRUIT OF THIS MYSTERY

Penance for our Sins

THE HOLY VIRGIN SAID, "As the Lord was brought to the pillar He was then dragged along the ground and thrown down so cruelly and violently that it knocked His head and broke His teeth. He was struck on His neck and cheek so forcefully that the sound of the blows reached my ears. At the command of the executioner He undressed Himself and freely hugged the pillar. He was bound with a rope and then scourged with barbed whips. The barbs caught in His skin and were then pulled backward, not just tearing but ploughing into Him so as to wound His whole body."

OUR FATHER   Our Father, Who art in Heaven, hallowed be Thy name, Thy kingdom come, Thy will be done, on earth as it is in heaven. Give us this day our daily bread; and forgive us our trespasses, as we forgive those who trespass against us; and lead us not into temptation, but deliver us from evil. Amen.

HAIL MARY (10)   Hail Mary, Full of Grace, the Lord is with thee. Blessed art thou among women and blessed is the fruit of thy womb, Jesus. Holy Mary, Mother of God, pray for us sinners now, and at the hour of our death. Amen.

1. May You be praised, my Lord Jesus Christ, for, like an innocent lamb, You most patiently permitted Yourself to be tied to the column and monstrously scourged; to be led, all bloody, to Pilate's judgment and there to be gazed at.

2. With what great meekness You suffered for us such cruel sorrows! You were so monstrously scourged and so injured with painful wounds that Your most innocent flesh and skin were all intolerably lacerated. Thus afflicted and aggrieved, You, O my most sweet Lord, stood, and, with patience and humility, awaited in extreme pain the hour of Your death.

3. Our Lady said, "When the time of my son's suffering arrived, His enemies seized Him and struck Him on the cheek and neck, spat at Him and ridiculed Him. Then He was led to the pillar of torture where He voluntarily removed

His clothes and placed His hands around the pillar, and His enemies mercilessly bound them."

4. "At the first blow, it was as though my heart had been pierced and I lost the use of my senses. Then, coming out of it, I saw His whole wounded body, for His body was naked during the scourging. When He stood bound at the pillar, He had no covering at all, but stood as naked as when He had been born, suffering the shame of His nakedness."

5. "Then all my son's friends fled from Him, and His enemies came together from all directions and stood there, scourging His body, which was pure from every stain and sin. I was standing nearby, and at the very first lashing, I fell down as if I were dead. When I regained consciousness, I saw His body whipped and scourged so badly that His ribs were visible! What was even more terrible, when the whip was pulled out, His flesh was furrowed and torn by it, just as the earth is by a plough! As my son was standing there, all bloody and wounded, so that no place could be found on Him that was still intact and no sound spot could be scourged, then someone present there, aroused in spirit, asked, 'Are you going to kill Him before He is even judged?' And he cut off His bonds immediately."

6. "Once released from the pillar, my son turned first to get His clothes, yet He was not given the time to put them on but was led away while still putting His arms into His sleeves. The footprints He left at the pillar were so full of blood that I could easily make them out and see which way they led by

the mark of His blood. And He wiped His bloody face with His tunic."

7. "At my son's passion I was like a woman whose heart was pierced by many spears. The first spear was His shameful nakedness, for I saw my most beloved and mighty son stand naked at the pillar without any clothing to cover Him at all. The second spear was the accusation against Him, for they accused Him of being a traitorous betrayer and liar, the One Whom I knew to be righteous and true and never to have offended or wished to offend or injure anyone. The third spear was His crown of thorns that pierced His sacred head so violently that the blood flowed down into His mouth and His beard and ears. My heart was pierced with as many spears as the arteries from which His most precious blood flowed out of Him."

8. Then the Son spoke, saying, "I was regarded as a worm, lying as though dead in the winter. Passers by spat on Me and kicked Me. On that day the Jews treated Me like a worm, for they held Me to be the lowest and most unworthy of creatures. But even now do Christians scorn me, for they regard as meaningless everything I have done and endured for them out of love. They trample Me down every time they fear and venerate man more than Me, their God, every time they count My judgment as nothing and fix the time and measure for My mercy according to their own conceptions."

9. Then the Son said to St. Bridget, "My bride, as you have sinned in all your limbs, so shall you also make satisfaction and penance in every limb. But, because of your good will

and your purpose of atoning for your sins, I shall change My justice into mercy by foregoing a painful punishment for a small penance. Therefore, embrace and take upon yourself a little hard work, so that you may be made clean of sin and reach the great reward sooner. If you are ashamed of being poor and despised, then consider how I, your God, walked before you, when My servants and friends abandoned Me in the world; for I was not seeking earthly friends, but heavenly friends. And if you now are troubled and afraid about the burden and difficulty of work and sickness, then consider how difficult and painful it is to burn in hell! What would you not deserve if you had offended an earthly master as you have Me?"

10. "Purify yourself constantly from sin, according to the advice of those I have entrusted you to. Hide no sin! Leave nothing unexamined! Do not consider any sin to be light or worthy of disregard! For anything you forget, I will remind you of and give judgement. None of the sins you have done will come before My judgment if they are punished and expiated through your penance while you live. But those sins for which you made no penance will be purged either in purgatory or by some secret judgment of Mine, unless you make a full satisfaction and amendment for them here in this world."

GLORY BE TO THE FATHER   Glory be to the Father, and to the Son, and to the Holy Spirit, as it was in the beginning, is now and ever shall be, world without end. Amen.

THE FATIMA PRAYER   O my Jesus, forgive us our sins, save us from the fires of hell, lead all souls to heaven, especially those in most need of Thy mercy.

The Crowning with Thorns

THE FRUIT OF THIS MYSTERY

A desire to see Christ enthroned, as the true king that He is

LORY BE TO YOU, my Lord Jesus Christ, for the derision that You endured while You stood invested with purple and crowned with the sharpest thorns. With great patience You endured the spitting on Your glorious face, the veiling of Your eyes, and, on Your cheek and neck, the grave and cutting blows of the deadly hands of the wicked.

OUR FATHER   Our Father, Who art in Heaven, hallowed be
Thy name, Thy kingdom come, Thy will be done, on earth as
it is in heaven. Give us this day our daily bread; and forgive us
our trespasses, as we forgive those who trespass against us; and
lead us not into temptation, but deliver us from evil. Amen.

HAIL MARY (10)   Hail Mary, Full of Grace, the Lord is
with thee. Blessed art thou among women and blessed is the
fruit of thy womb, Jesus. Holy Mary, Mother of God, pray
for us sinners now, and at the hour of our death. Amen.

1. The Son of God said, "O My enemies, abominable, ungrate-
ful and degenerate, I seem to you, as it were, a worm lying on
the ground in winter. Therefore, you do whatever things you
will, and you prosper. Therefore, I will arise in summer and
then you shall be silent, and you shall not escape My hand.
But nevertheless, O My enemies, because I have redeemed
you with My blood and because I am in quest of naught but
your souls, therefore return to Me even now with humility
and I will gladly receive you as My children. Shake off from
you the devil's heavy yoke and recall My charity and you shall
see in your conscience that I am sweet and meek."

2. The Blessed Mother said, "Then My son put His clothes
back on, and I saw that the place where He had been standing was filled with blood! By observing my son's footprints,
I could see where He had walked because the ground was
bloody there as well. They did not even wait for Him to get
dressed, but pushed and dragged Him to make Him hurry
up. While my son was being led away like a robber, He wiped
the blood from His eyes."

3. May You be blessed, my Lord Jesus Christ. You were led to Caiaphas, and You, Who are the Judge of all, humbly permitted Yourself to be given over to the judgment of Pilate. From Pilate the judge, You were sent to Herod; and You permitted Yourself to be mocked and scorned by him; and then You consented to be returned again to be judged by Pilate.

4. Our Divine Lord said, "And if a follower of Mine is despised by men, then he should think how I, God, was despised, taunted and suffered it patiently, how I was judged and spoke not; how I was scourged and crowned with thorns, and did not complain. My disciple must also take heed that he show no tokens of wrath or impatience to them who taunt him or despise him; but he ought to bless them who persecute him, so that they who see it may bless God, Whom My disciple professes to follow; and indeed, God Himself shall return blessings for their curses."

5. May You be blessed, my Lord Jesus Christ. Most patiently, in Pilate's presence, with Your own blessed ears You willed to hear abuse and lies hurled at You and the voices of the people asking that the guilty robber be acquitted and that You, the innocent, be condemned.

6. The Lord said, "Behold, My bride, what kind of people they are! I made them, and could destroy and damn them with a word if I wanted to. How bold and arrogant they are toward Me! But because of the prayers of My mother and of all the saints, I am still so merciful and patient that I will send them the words of My mouth and offer them My mercy. If they want to accept it, I will be appeased. Otherwise, they

will come to know My justice and be publicly humiliated like thieves in front of all angels and men, and be judged by every one of them. For just as the men who are hanged on gallows are devoured by ravens, they will also be devoured by demons, yet not die."

7. O Jesus, You were despoiled of Your garments and clothed in those of derision. Your face and eyes were veiled. You were buffeted, crowned with thorns and a reed was placed in Your hands. You were crushed with blows and overwhelmed with affronts and outrages.

8. The Lord said, "Why have you neglected My passion? Why do you not attend in your hearts to how I stood naked at the pillar, was bound and cruelly scourged with hard whips, and how I cried out, full of wounds and clothed in blood? And when you paint and anoint your faces, why do you not look at My face and see how it was full of blood? You are not even attentive to My eyes and how they grew dark and were covered with blood and tears, and how My eyelids turned blue. Therefore, know for very certain that as often as you daub your faces with makeup and other extraneous colouring, some of the infusion of the Holy Spirit is diminished in you and the devil draws nearer to you. In fact, as often as you adorn yourselves in disorderly and indecent clothing and so deform your bodies, the adornment of your souls is diminished and the devil's power is increased."

9. "I am like a great and mighty king. Four things belong to a king: First, he must be rich; second, generous; third, wise and fourth, charitable. I am in truth the King of the angels

and of all humanity. I also have those four qualities that I mentioned: First, I am the richest of all, for I give to everyone according to their needs but possess after this donation no less than before. Second, I am the most generous, since I am ready to give to anyone who prays with love for My mercy. Third, I am the wisest of all, since I know what is best for each and everyone. And fourth, I am charitable, since I am more ready to give than anyone is to ask."

10. My Lord Jesus Christ, You are truly the head of all men and angels, the worthy King of Kings and Lord of Lords; and You do all Your works out of true and ineffable charity. You humbly permitted Your blessed head to be crowned with a crown of thorns. Therefore may Your head and hair be truly blessed; and may they be gloriously adorned with an imperial diadem. May heaven and earth and sea and all things created be subject and obedient to Your empire and Your power unto eternity.

GLORY BE TO THE FATHER   Glory be to the Father, and to the Son, and to the Holy Spirit, as it was in the beginning, is now and ever shall be, world without end. Amen.

THE FATIMA PRAYER   O my Jesus, forgive us our sins, save us from the fires of hell, lead all souls to heaven, especially those in most need of Thy mercy.

The Carrying of the Cross

THE FRUIT OF THIS MYSTERY

Compassion for the sufferings of Our Blessed Redeemer

UR LADY SAW HIM led out, bound as a criminal, to a traitor's death. She saw Him struggling to carry His Cross, dragged forward and whipped as He stumbled, led like some wild beast rather than a lamb to the slaughter. As Isaiah had foretold, He went meekly to His death; like the lamb that is led to the slaughter house, like the sheep that is dumb before its shearers. Christ was patient in His sufferings. Mary endured patiently the sorrow of His sufferings. She followed Him, even to the place of death. She saw the wounds of His scourging, the crown of thorns, His cheeks disfigured with blows, His face covered with blood, and she wept in sorrow.

OUR FATHER   Our Father, Who art in Heaven, hallowed be Thy name, Thy kingdom come, Thy will be done, on earth as it is in heaven. Give us this day our daily bread; and forgive us our trespasses, as we forgive those who trespass against us; and lead us not into temptation, but deliver us from evil. Amen.

HAIL MARY (10)   Hail Mary, Full of Grace, the Lord is with thee. Blessed art thou among women and blessed is the fruit of thy womb, Jesus. Holy Mary, Mother of God, pray for us sinners now, and at the hour of our death. Amen.

1. May You be honoured, my Lord Jesus Christ. With Your glorious body covered in gore, the judgment on You was the death of the cross. The cross You bore in pain on Your sacred shoulders; and, amidst frenzy, You were led to the place of Your passion. Despoiled of Your garments, thus You willed to be fixed to the wood of the cross.

2. The Blessed Mother said, "When He had been sentenced to death, they placed the cross on Him so that He could carry it to the place of suffering. When He had carried it for a while, a man, Simon, came along and took the cross to carry it for Him. As my son was going to the place of suffering, some people hit Him on the neck, while others hit Him in the face. He was so brutally and forcefully beaten that, although I did

not see who hit Him, I heard the sound of the blow clearly. When I reached the place of suffering with Him, I saw all the instruments of his death lying there ready."

3. My Lord Jesus Christ, You are worthily called a leader by all, because You bore on Your holy shoulders and neck the burdensome bulk of the cross. In doing so, You mightily shattered the gates of hell and led the souls of the elect back to heaven. Therefore, to Your blessed neck and shoulders that endured such pain, be honour and glory eternally without end.

4. My Lord Jesus Christ, the servants of this world gladly expose their own lives to death in war in order that their lords may enjoy safety of life; but You, O my good Lord, quickly hastened to the death of the cross in order that Your servants might not miserably perish. And so it is just that You are eternally adored by all your servants, whom You have thus delivered.

5. My Lord Jesus Christ, may Your precious ribs and Your back be blessed and honoured unto eternity by all human beings who sweat over labours spiritual and earthly. For from Your infancy even to your death, You laboured unceasingly for our redemption; and with great pain and burdensomeness, You bore our sins on Your back.

6. The Virgin said, "While I was at Mount Calvary, most mournfully weeping, I saw that my Lord, Who was naked and scourged, had been led by the Jews to His crucifixion. He was being guarded by them diligently. The crucifiers were nearby, and ready to work their cruelty."

7. "Then my hands became numb, my eyes were darkened, and my face became pale as a corpse. My ears could hear nothing, my mouth could not speak, my feet trembled, and my body fell to the ground. When I got up from the ground and saw my son looking horribly disfigured and more miserable than a leper, I submitted my entire will to His knowing with certainty that everything had happened according to His will and could not have happened unless He had allowed it. I therefore thanked Him for everything, and so there was always some joy mixed with my sadness, because I saw that He, Who had never sinned, had, in His great love, wanted to suffer this much for the sins of mankind. Therefore, may all those who are in the world contemplate how I suffered during the hours of my son's passion and always have it in front of their eyes and in their thoughts!"

8. "On being ordered, He lay down with His back to the cross and, when He was asked to do so, first stretched out His right hand. Then, since His left hand could not reach the other corner of the cross, it had to be stretched out at full length. His feet were similarly stretched out to reach the slots for the nails and placed crosswise, and, as if they had been loosened from the shinbones, were fastened to the wood of the cross by two nails driven through solid bone, as had been done with His hands. At the first hammer stroke, I was thrown into a stupor of sorrow, and when I awoke I saw my son already fastened to the cross. I heard men saying to one another, 'What has this man committed, theft, robbery, or fraud?' Others answered that He was a fraud. Then the crown of thorns was pushed down on His head so hard that it came down to the middle of His forehead. Streams of blood poured

down from where the thorns sat and filled His face and hair and eyes and beard so that almost nothing at all but blood could be seen. He could not even see me standing there by the cross without blinking to get rid of the blood."

9. St. Bridget explained, "Those savage torturers monstrously crucified His right hand, piercing it with a nail through that part where the bone was more solid. And then, with a rope, they pulled violently on His left hand and fastened it to the cross in the same manner. Finally, they extended His body on the cross beyond all measure; and placing one of His shins on top of the other, they fastened to the cross His feet with two nails. They violently extended those glorious limbs so far on the cross that nearly all of His veins and sinews were bursting."

10. "Then the crown of thorns, which they had removed from His head when He was being crucified, they now put back, fitting it onto His most holy head. It pricked His noble head with such force that then and there His eyes were filled with flowing blood and His ears were obstructed. And His face and beard were covered as if they had been dipped in that rose-red blood. And at once those crucifiers and soldiers quickly removed all the planks that abutted the cross, and then the cross remained alone and lofty, and my Lord was crucified upon it."

GLORY BE TO THE FATHER   Glory be to the Father, and to the Son, and to the Holy Spirit, as it was in the beginning, is now and ever shall be, world without end. Amen.

THE FATIMA PRAYER   O my Jesus, forgive us our sins, save us from the fires of hell, lead all souls to heaven, especially those in most need of Thy mercy.

The Crucifixion of Our Lord

*A continual spirit of reparation for the ungratefulness of
sinners towards the passion of their redeemer*

ARY, HIS BLESSED MOTHER, saw Him stretched on
the Cross, and heard the blows of the hammer as
the nails pierced His hands and feet. So great was
her suffering and sorrow that her strength almost failed her
as she stood by and watched. She saw the vinegar and gall
offered for His lips to taste. and her own lips could not move

in prayer. She heard His cry "My God, My God, why have You forsaken Me?", and saw His head fall forward and His body become rigid as He breathed forth His spirit. She stood and saw how He died. Then truly was her heart quite pierced by the sword of sorrow. It was the strength God gave that alone saved her from dying in such sorrow. To see her son, stripped and bleeding, dying, pierced by a lance, mocked by those who stood by, jeered at by soldiers, deserted by all but a few of His chosen ones, abandoned by so many whom He had won to justice and truth, to see this most bitter death, could there be sorrow as deep as hers?

OUR FATHER   Our Father, Who art in Heaven, hallowed be Thy name, Thy kingdom come, Thy will be done, on earth as it is in heaven. Give us this day our daily bread; and forgive us our trespasses, as we forgive those who trespass against us; and lead us not into temptation, but deliver us from evil. Amen.

HAIL MARY (10)   Hail Mary, Full of Grace, the Lord is with thee. Blessed art thou among women and blessed is the fruit of thy womb, Jesus. Holy Mary, Mother of God, pray for us sinners now, and at the hour of our death. Amen.

1. Mary said, "I was also the one closest to Him at His suffering and I was never separated from Him. I stood very near His cross, and because that which is closest to the heart stings the worst, so seeing His pain was heavier and worse for me than for others. When He looked at me from the cross and I saw Him, then tears flowed from my eyes like blood from veins. And when He saw me so stricken with pain and overwhelming sorrow, He felt such a sorrow over my pain that all the pain

of His own wounds became as subsided and dead for the sake of the pain He saw in me. I can therefore boldly say that His pain was my pain since His heart was my heart. For just as Adam and Eve sold the world for an apple, so my son and I bought back the world as with one heart. Consider therefore, my daughter, how I was at the death of my son, and it will not be hard for you to give up the world and her cares."

2. O Jesus! Heavenly Physician, raised aloft on the Cross to heal our wounds with Yours. Remember the bruises which You suffered and the weakness of all Your members which were swollen to such a degree that never was there pain like Yours. From the crown of Your head to the soles of Your feet, there was not one spot on Your Body that was not in torment and yet, forgetting all Your sufferings, You did not cease to pray to Your Heavenly Father for Your enemies saying, "Father, forgive them, for they know not what they do." Through Your Great Mercy, may the remembrance of Your Most Bitter Passion effect in us a perfect contrition and the remission of all our sins.

3. St. Bridget said, "And as I, filled with sorrow, gazed at their cruelty, I then saw His most mournful mother lying on the earth, as if trembling and half dead. She was being consoled by John and by those others, her sisters, who were then standing not far from the cross on its right side. Then the new sorrow of the compassion of that most holy mother so transfixed me that I felt, as it were, that a sharp sword of unbearable bitterness was piercing my heart. Then at last His sorrowful Mother arose; and, as it were, in a state of physical exhaustion, she looked at her son. Thus, supported by her

sisters, she stood there all dazed and in suspense, as though dead yet living, transfixed by the sword of sorrow. When her son saw her and His other friends weeping, with a tearful voice He commended her to John. It was quite discernible in His bearing and voice that out of compassion for His Mother, His own heart was being penetrated by a most sharp arrow of sorrow beyond all measure. When His death drew near, His heart burst because of the violence of the pain. His whole body convulsed, and His head raised itself a little, and then dropped down again. His mouth was open and His tongue was completely bloody. His hands retracted a little from the place of the nail holes, and His feet were made to bear more of the weight of his body. His fingers and arms were stretched out somewhat, and His back was tightly pressed against the cross.

4. The Blessed Virgin explained, "After He had entrusted me to His disciple, He lifted up His head, raised His weeping eyes to heaven, and cried out with a voice from deep within His chest, saying, 'My God, My God, why have You abandoned Me?' Never was I able to forget that cry, not until I came to heaven, the cry that He uttered, moved more by my suffering than by His own. Now the colour of death appeared in those parts of His body that were visible beneath the blood. His cheeks cleaved to His teeth. You could count His thin, naked ribs. His stomach, emptied now of all its juices, was sucked in toward His back, and even His nostrils looked thin now. When His heart was near to breaking, His whole body shook and His beard fell toward His chest. Right then, I collapsed lifeless to the ground. His mouth remained open, as He had already breathed His last. His tongue and teeth and the blood in his mouth were visible to onlookers. His half-closed eyes

had rolled backward. His now dead body sagged downward, with His knees bent to either side, and His feet bending on the nails like hinges."

5. St. Bridget said, "Then, therefore, in distress from the exceeding anguish of His pain and already near to death, He cried to the Father in a loud and tearful voice. He then had pale lips, a bloody tongue and a sunken abdomen that adhered to his back as if He had no organs within. A second time also, He cried out again in the greatest of pain and anxiety, "O Father, into Your hands I commend My spirit." Then His head, raising itself a little, immediately bowed; and thus He sent forth His spirit. When His mother saw these things, she trembled at that immense bitterness and would have fallen onto the earth if she had not been supported by the other women."

6. Our Lady explained, "Meanwhile other people standing nearby were saying almost insultingly to me, 'O, Mary, your son is dead.' Others, more noble minded, said, 'Lady, your son's suffering is now ended, He passes into glory.' A little later, after His side had been opened, the lance was pulled out with blood that was brown in colour showing on its tip, which meant that the lance had pierced His heart. That penetrating lance was also felt going through my own heart, and it is a wonder that my heart did not burst. Though the others were going away, I could not go away. I felt almost comforted to be able to touch His body when it was taken down from the cross, and take it in my arms, and clean His wounds and wipe away the blood. I closed His mouth with my fingers and shut His eyes as well. I could not bend His

rigid arms all the way back to repose on His chest but only across His stomach. His knees could not be straightened out but pointed outward in the same position in which they had stiffened on the cross."

7. St. Bridget said, "The Jews standing around cried out in mockery against His mother, saying many things. And while the crowds were thus standing about, one man came running with the greatest of fury and fixed a lance in His right side with such violence and force that the lance would have passed almost through the other side of the body. Thus, when the lance was extracted from the body, at once a stream, as it were, of blood spurted out of that wound in abundance; in fact, the iron blade of the lance and a part of the shaft came out of the body red and stained with the blood. Seeing these things, His mother so violently trembled with bitter sighing that it was quite discernible in her face and bearing that her soul was then being penetrated by the sharp sword of sorrow."

8. "When all these things had been accomplished and when the large crowds were receding, certain of the Lord's friends took Him down. Then, with pity, His mother received Him into her most holy arms; and sitting, she laid Him on her knee, all torn as He was and wounded and black and blue. Others, the weeping women, washed Him. And then, with her linen cloth, His most mournful mother wiped His whole body and its wounds. She closed His eyes and kissed them; and she wrapped Him in a clean cloth of fine linen. And thus they escorted Him with lamentation and very great sorrow and placed Him in the sepulchre. And Mary said to me, 'I would willingly have been placed alive in the grave with my

son if it had been His will! O my daughter, see what my son has endured for you, and love Him with all your heart!'"

9. We read that once, when the Ark of God fell into the hands of enemies, the wife of one of God's priests died for sorrow. How much greater was the sorrow of Mary, for she saw the body of her son, which the Ark prefigured, nailed to the wood of the Cross. Her love for her son was love for the Son of God, greater than the loves of all men. If the loss of the Ark could cause sorrow and death, the death of Christ would have brought Mary to death but for God's gift to support so grievous a sorrow. By His death, Christ opened the gateway to heaven, and won for His followers their entry into joy. Mary looked up from the depths of her sorrow, as one coming back from the gates of death. No words or works of men were so powerful to bring men to God. Many lost faith when they saw Christ die. She alone withstood the unbelief of men, seeing in Christ her Son the Son of God, over Whose Godhead death could have no dominion.

10. Our Lady said, "You should reflect on five things, my daughter. First, how every limb in my son's body grew stiff and cold at His death and how the blood that flowed from His wounds as He was suffering dried up and clung to each limb. Second, how His heart was pierced so bitterly and mercilessly that the man speared it until the lance hit a rib, and both parts of the heart were on the lance. Third, reflect on how He was taken down from the cross! The two men who took Him down from the cross made use of three stepladders: one reached to His feet, the second just below His armpits and arms, the third to the middle of His body. The first man

got up and held Him by the middle. The second, getting up on another ladder, first pulled a nail out of one arm, then moved the ladder and pulled the nail from the other hand. The nails extended through the crossbeam. The man who had been holding up the weight of the body then went down as slowly and carefully as he could, while the other man got up on the stepladder that went to the feet and pulled out the nails from the feet. When He was lowered to the ground, one of them held the body by the head and the other by the feet. I, His mother, held Him about the waist. And so the three of us carried Him to a rock that I had covered with a clean sheet and in that we wrapped His body. I did not sew the sheet together, because I knew that He would not decay in the grave.

GLORY BE TO THE FATHER   Glory be to the Father, and to the Son, and to the Holy Spirit, as it was in the beginning, is now and ever shall be, world without end. Amen.

THE FATIMA PRAYER   O my Jesus, forgive us our sins, save us from the fires of hell, lead all souls to heaven, especially those in most need of Thy mercy.

CONCLUDING PRAYERS   *Upon completing the recitation of the Holy Rosary, the following prayers are customary, but others too may be added according to one's devotion and preference.*

HAIL HOLY QUEEN   Hail Holy Queen, Mother of Mercy, hail our life, our sweetness and our hope. To thee do we cry, poor banished children of Eve, to thee do we send up our sighs, mourning and weeping in this vale of tears. Turn then, most gracious advocate, thine eyes of mercy towards us, and after this, our exile, show unto us the blessed fruit of thy womb, Jesus. O clement, O loving, O sweet Virgin Mary. Pray for us O holy Mother of God, that we may be made worthy of the promises of Christ.

Let Us Pray   O God, Whose only begotten son, by His life, death and resurrection, has purchased for us the rewards of eternal life, grant we beseech Thee, that meditating on these mysteries of the most Holy Rosary of the Blessed Virgin Mary, we may both imitate what they contain and obtain what they promise, through the same Christ our Lord. Amen.

PRAYER TO SAINT MICHAEL THE ARCHANGEL   Holy Michael, the Archangel, defend us in the day of battle. Be our safeguard against the wickedness and snares of the devil. May God rebuke him, we humbly pray; and do thou, O Prince of the heavenly hosts, by the power of God thrust down into hell Satan and all the evil spirits who wander through the world seeking the ruin of souls. Amen.

MEMORARE   Remember, O most gracious Virgin Mary, that never was it known that anyone who fled to thy protection, implored thy help, or sought thine intercession was left unaided. Inspired by this confidence, I fly unto thee, O Virgin of virgins, my mother; to thee do I come, before thee I stand, sinful and sorrowful. O Mother of the Word Incarnate, despise not my petitions, but in thy mercy hear and answer me. Amen.

May the Divine Assistance remain always with us, and may the souls of the faithful departed, through the mercy of God rest in peace. Amen.

The Glorious Mysteries

The Resurrection

THE FRUIT OF THIS MYSTERY

Sharing in Our Lady's Joy at the resurrection of her son

HEN THE THIRD DAY came, it brought bewilderment and anxiety to the disciples. The women going to the tomb to anoint the body of Jesus sought Him and could not find Him. The Apostles were gathered together in their fear, guarding the doors. Then, surely, though we are not told of this in the Gospels, Mary spoke of the resurrection of her son, that He had truly risen from death, that He was

73

alive again in all His humanity, no more subject to death, risen to an eternal glory. We read that Mary Magdalen and the Apostles were first to see the risen Christ. But we may believe that Mary His mother knew of his rising before all others, and that she was the first to see Him.

OUR FATHER   Our Father, Who art in Heaven, hallowed be Thy name, Thy kingdom come, Thy will be done, on earth as it is in heaven. Give us this day our daily bread; and forgive us our trespasses, as we forgive those who trespass against us; and lead us not into temptation, but deliver us from evil. Amen.

HAIL MARY (10)   Hail Mary, Full of Grace, the Lord is with thee. Blessed art thou among women and blessed is the fruit of thy womb, Jesus. Holy Mary, Mother of God, pray for us sinners now, and at the hour of our death. Amen.

1. Our Lady, the Virgin Mary, said, "I can truly say that there were two hearts in the one grave where my son was buried. Is it not said, 'Where your treasure is, there will your heart be also'? Likewise, my heart and mind were constantly going to my son's grave. At my son's burial were Mary Magdalene and the other holy women. Angels, too, as many as the atoms of the sun, were there, showing their allegiance to their Creator. I was like a woman giving birth who shakes in every limb of her body after delivery. Although she can scarcely breathe due to the pain, still she rejoices inwardly as much as she can because she knows that the child she has given birth to will never return to the same painful ordeal he has just left. In the same way, although no sorrow could compare with my sorrow

over the death of my son, still I rejoiced in my soul because I knew my son would no longer die but would live forever.

2. May you be blessed, my Lady, O Virgin Mary. You parted from the sepulchre of your son and, all full of grief, were brought by His friends to the house of John. But there, at once, you felt a relief of your great sorrow because you most surely foreknew that your son would quickly rise.

3. Her faith never faltered that Christ would rise again, and in this faith she could comfort many whose faith had failed. They took Him down from the cross, and wrapped Him in fine linen with spices, and laid Him in the tomb. Then all left. Few still had faith that He would rise. Little by little, the sorrows of Mary's heart lightened, and she felt the first sweetness of consolation. The sufferings of her son were at an end. She knew that on the third day He would rise, would rise with His humanity united again to His divinity, would rise to everlasting honour and glory, to suffer and to die no more.

4. Rejoice, my most worthy Lady, O Virgin Mary, for in the same instant that your son arose from death He willed to make this same fact known to you, His most Blessed Mother. Then and there He appeared to you by Himself, and later He showed to other persons that He was the One Who had been raised from death after having endured death in His own living body.

5. May You be blessed, my Lord Jesus Christ. You hung dead on the wood of the cross, and straight away You mightily liberated Your friends from the prison of hell. And then, on the

third day, You rose from the dead, and You showed Yourself alive to as many as it pleased You.

6. The Lord asked, "Was My body that Thomas touched after My resurrection a spiritual or corporeal body? If it was corporeal, how did it pass through the locked doors? But, if it was spiritual, how was it visible to corporeal eyes?" The answer was given, "You were both corporeal and spiritual after rising from the dead. It is because of the eternal power of Your divinity and because of a special privilege of Your glorified flesh that You can enter anywhere and be present everywhere."

7. The Lord asked, "Is it more difficult or more miraculous for Me to perform a miracle now than it was when I was on earth? If My glorified flesh could pass through the locked doors then, why can it not be in the hands of the priests now? My daughter, believe that I am the Christ, the Restorer of Life, the True One, the very truth itself and not a liar, I am the eternal power without which nothing ever was or ever shall be."

8. The Lord asked, "If My divine power had been revealed openly for all to see as I was dying, who would have dared to take Me down from the cross and bury Me? Do you not see that it would have been easy for Me to have come down from the cross and to have destroyed My crucifiers, but how then would the prophecy of My resurrection have been fulfilled, or how then would My virtue of patience have been shown forth? In order to set the captives free, I, Who was free, made Myself captive; and in order to save the guilty, I, Who was guiltless, stood steadfast on the cross."

9. The Lord said, "How then should they deserve to enter into My glory who have little faith, vain hope, and no love? If they believed in the eternal joy of heaven and in the horrific torments of hell, they would desire nothing but Me. If they had a firm and steadfast hope, then their every thought and desire would be directed toward Me. If they had a divine love for Me, then they would at least think in their soul about what I did for their sake. But their faith is sick and wavering and their love for Me is completely cold. Therefore they do not deserve to be heard or to enter into My glory since they do not want to follow their Lord in suffering, and, therefore, they should not follow Him to the glory."

10. Body and soul we shall stand before God, for in all things, body and soul act as one. Christ's sinless body rose from the dead, and is now and for ever united in glory with His Divinity. The justice of God has willed that we must rise, body and soul, at the last day, to be repaid for our works.

GLORY BE TO THE FATHER   Glory be to the Father, and to the Son, and to the Holy Spirit, as it was in the beginning, is now and ever shall be, world without end. Amen.

THE FATIMA PRAYER   O my Jesus, forgive us our sins, save us from the fires of hell, lead all souls to heaven, especially those in most need of Thy mercy.

The Ascension

MAY YOU BE BLESSED and praised and glorified unto the ages, my Lord Jesus. You sit upon the throne in Your kingdom of heaven, in the glory of Your divinity, corporeally alive, with all Your most holy limbs that You took from the flesh of the Virgin. In this same appearance You will come on the day of judgment to judge the souls of all the living and the dead, You, Who live and reign with the Father and the Holy Spirit unto ages of ages.

OUR FATHER   Our Father, Who art in Heaven, hallowed be Thy name, Thy kingdom come, Thy will be done, on earth as it is in heaven. Give us this day our daily bread; and forgive us our trespasses, as we forgive those who trespass against us; and lead us not into temptation, but deliver us from evil. Amen.

HAIL MARY (10)   Hail Mary, Full of Grace, the Lord is with thee. Blessed art thou among women and blessed is the fruit of thy womb, Jesus. Holy Mary, Mother of God, pray for us sinners now, and at the hour of our death. Amen.

1. The Lord Jesus Christ said, "I am like a powerful lord who built a great city and named it after himself. Thereafter, he built a castle in the city in which there were many rooms for storing all kinds of useful necessities. Then, when he had built the castle and arranged all his things, he spoke to his people, saying, 'I am going away to a far away country. Stand firm and work manfully for my glory! I have made arrangements for your food and your necessities, and you have judges to judge you and defenders to defend you from your enemies.'"

2. The Queen of Heaven said, "It was from the Mount of Olives that my son flew in His human nature like an eagle to heaven where He ever was according to His divine nature. He was then renewed and rested according to His human nature, although He was always at rest and always the same according to His divine nature."

3. Rejoice therefore, my most worthy Lady, O Virgin Mary. On the fortieth day after His resurrection, you saw your son, in the sight of many, ascend with honour to His kingdom in heaven as Himself a king, accompanied by angels.

4. The Lord said, "I opened the gate of heaven with My heart's blood, and I illumined the way by My words and deeds, and at that moment when I opened heaven, the devil was deprived of that justice which he seemed to have; and those souls that were worthy were saved and freed. Then indeed the law was established that it should be in man's decision to follow Me, his God, in order to obtain the everlasting crown. But if he follows the devil's desires, he will have everlasting punishment. Thus the devil and I are in a struggle, in that we both desire souls as bridegrooms desire their brides. For I desire souls in order to give them eternal joy and honour; but the devil desires to give them eternal horror and sorrow."

5. My Lord Jesus Christ, Your blessed body is unceasingly praised and glorified by the harmonious jubilee of the citizens of heaven above. I too, a person unwise and unworthy, desire with all my heart, and with all my mouth, to offer to all the members of Your precious body as much honour, thanks and praise as I am able.

6. St. Bridget said, "I saw a grand palace like the serene sky. In it was the host of the heavenly army, innumerable as the atoms of the sun and having a gleam as of the sun's rays. But in the palace, on a wonderful throne there sat, as it were, the person of a human being. It was the Lord, robed in

incomprehensible beauty and immense power. His clothes were wonderful and of inexpressible brightness."

7. The Lord said to the saint, "Although My human form seems to be here before you and to be speaking with you, nonetheless it is truer to say that your soul and your conscience are with Me and in Me. Nothing in heaven or on earth is impossible or difficult for Me. I am like a powerful king who comes to a city with his troops and takes up the whole place, occupying all of it. In like manner, My grace fills all of your limbs and strengthens them all. I am within you and without you. Although I may be speaking with you, I remain the same in My glory. What could possibly be difficult for Me Who sustains all things with My power and arranges all things in My wisdom, surpassing everything in excellence?"

8. God is like a man who hangs a golden crown outside the door of his house and cries out to passers by, "Anyone of any social standing can earn this crown! He who is most nobly clothed in virtue will obtain it." Know that if bishops and rulers are wise in worldly wisdom, God is wiser than them in a spiritual sense, for He raises up the humble and does not give His approval to the proud. That is why many persons through their good intentions attain the spiritual rank of honour that was scorned by those who were called to it in a physical sense.

9. The Lord said, "You are wondering why you have heard that a certain friend of God, who should be esteemed, is suffering hardships, while, on the other hand, you have heard that a certain enemy of God, who you thought should be

whipped, has been honoured. I answer, what is the suffering of the world if not a kind of preparation and elevation to the crown of reward? And what does worldly prosperity mean for someone who abuses grace if not a kind of descent into perdition? To suffer in the world is truly an ascension to life. But, for the unrighteous, prospering in the world is truly a descent into hell. The Lord wishes to test and see who is fit to enter into the city of glory. He gives a higher crown of glory to all those He has seen to be more vigilant in the contest."

10. "I am like a lord who is both father and judge. When he goes forth to judge, the bystanders say to him, 'Lord, proceed quickly and make your judgment!' Their lord answers them, 'Wait a little until tomorrow, because perhaps my son will still amend himself in the meantime.' When he comes back the next day, the people say to him, 'Proceed, lord, and make your judgment! Why are you postponing the judgment for so long and do not judge the guilty?' Their lord answers them, 'Wait a little while longer, to see if my son betters himself, and if he then does not repent, I shall make a just judgment over him.' In this way I patiently endure mankind even until the last moment, since I am both Father and Judge. But My justice is unchangeable, and even though it sometimes is postponed a long time, I will still either punish sinners who do not better themselves or show them mercy if they amend themselves."

GLORY BE TO THE FATHER   Glory be to the Father, and to the Son, and to the Holy Spirit, as it was in the beginning, is now and ever shall be, world without end. Amen.

THE FATIMA PRAYER   O my Jesus, forgive us our sins, save us from the fires of hell, lead all souls to heaven, especially those in most need of Thy mercy.

The Descent of the Holy Spirit

THE FRUIT OF THIS MYSTERY

A desire to share the one true faith with others

XULT, MY MOST WORTHY Lady, O Virgin Mary. You merited to see how, after His Ascension, your son suddenly transmitted to His apostles and disciples the Holy Spirit with which He had previously filled you to the full. By increasing the fervour of their charity and the rightness of their Catholic belief, He wonderfully enlightened their hearts.

OUR FATHER   Our Father, Who art in Heaven, hallowed be Thy name, Thy kingdom come, Thy will be done, on earth as it is in heaven. Give us this day our daily bread; and forgive us our trespasses, as we forgive those who trespass against us; and lead us not into temptation, but deliver us from evil. Amen.

HAIL MARY (10)   Hail Mary, Full of Grace, the Lord is with thee. Blessed art thou among women and blessed is the fruit of thy womb, Jesus. Holy Mary, Mother of God, pray for us sinners now, and at the hour of our death. Amen.

1. I, God, am spirit. I speak, and it is done. I command, and all obey me. I am truly He Who gives being and life to all, Who, before making the sky and the mountains and the earth, exist in Myself, Who am above and beyond all things, Who am within all things, and all things are in Me, and without Me there is nothing. The Divine Spirit blows when and where He wills, and can do all things, and knows all things, and is swifter and more agile than all other spirits. The Holy Spirit possesses every power, and, seeing beforehand all things present, past, and future, comprehends all things."

2. Rejoice still more, my Lady, O Virgin Mary; and at your joy, let all the world rejoice. For many years after His Ascension your son permitted you to remain in this world for the consolation of His friends and for the strengthening of the faith, for the relief of the poor and for the sound counselling of the apostles. Then, through your prudent words, your seemly behaviour, and your virtuous deeds, your son converted countless Jews and infidel pagans to the Catholic faith; and by wondrously illuminating them, He enlightened them to

confess that you are a virgin-mother and that He, your son, is God with a true human nature.

3. The Holy Virgin spoke to the Son and said, "May You be blessed, my son and my God, Lord of Angels and King of glory! I beg of You that the words that You have spoken may take root in the hearts of Your friends and that their minds may cling as firmly to these words as the pitch with which Noah's ark was plastered, which neither storm-waves nor winds could break and dissolve. May they be spread out all over the world like branches and sweet flowers whose fragrance is spread far and wide, in order that they also may bear fruit and become sweet like the date, the sweetness of which delights the soul exceedingly much."

4. The Lord said, "My Spirit descended over the apostles on the day of Pentecost and inflamed them so that they spoke in the language of all peoples. Let My friends see to it that My words reach My enemies, so that they, perhaps, convert themselves and feel sorrow and remorse for their sins, when their peril and My judgment are made known to them."

5. The Lord said to His intimate friend, "I opened your spiritual eyes so that you might see spiritual things. I opened your ears so that you might hear the things that are of the Spirit. I will show you a likeness of My body as it was during and before My passion, and such as it was after the resurrection, as Magdalene and Peter and others saw it. You will also hear My voice as it spoke to Moses from within the bush. This same voice is now speaking within your soul."

6. Our Lady said, "When I see blowing on the hearts of human beings the dangerous winds of the devil's temptations and wicked suggestions, at once I have recourse to my Lord and my God, my son Jesus Christ, helping them with my prayers and obtaining from Him His outpouring of the holy infusion of the Holy Spirit. He enters their hearts to prop them up and savingly confirms them that they may be kept spiritually uninjured by the diabolic wind of temptations lest the devil prevail against them, breaking their souls and plucking them up by the stem in accord with his wicked desire."

7. Then Truth Himself spoke and said, "I, in My Godhead, took manhood of a Virgin, in which manhood I spoke and preached to people. I also sent the Holy Spirit to the Apostles, and I spoke by their tongues. Now I speak each day by spiritual infusion to those I chose. But My friends, know that I Who am Truth Itself, often speak My words into a soul, only to have them despised."

8. When Christ ascended to the glory of His kingdom, the Virgin Mary remained on earth. We cannot know what her presence meant to so many. Those who loved God were strengthened in their love; those who had turned from Him were brought back to His love. The Apostles looked to her for guidance and counsel. The Martyrs found in her courage to face suffering and death. The Confessors of the Faith were strengthened in their believing. Virgins were drawn to her purity. Widows were consoled by her sorrows. Husbands and wives found in her a pattern of perfection. All who heard and obeyed the word of God found in Mary great comfort and help. Whenever the Apostles came to her, she was able

to teach them about Christ, and help them to understand. The Martyrs remembered the long years of sorrow borne so patiently by Mary His Mother, and they bore their martyrdom even more readily. The Confessors, meditating on Mary, learnt many things about the truths of the Faith. From her example, they learnt too the wise use of earthly things, food, drink and sleep, work and rest. Virgins learnt from Mary's example true chastity in virtue. They learnt too the wise use of their time, how to avoid vanity and foolish talk, and see all things in the light of true holiness. Widows learnt from her, consolation in sorrow, strength against temptation, and humble submission to God's will.

9. The Son spoke through the bride to a certain priest, telling him, "You are like an immobile mill wheel. When it stands fixed and does not move, then the grain does not get ground in the mill. This wheel signifies your will. It should be mobile not with respect to your own will and desire but to Mine, and you ought to surrender yourself completely into My hands. However, this wheel is very immobile toward My will, since the water of earthly consideration is troubling your mind too much. The contemplation of My works and My passion is almost dead in your heart, for which reason you have no feeling or taste for the food of the soul. So break through the obstacle that obstructs the passage of the water! Let the water flow so that it makes the wheel turn and become mobile again so that the grain can be easily ground. The obstacle holding back the water is mental pride and ambition. These obstruct the grace of the Holy Spirit and impede all the good fruit that the soul should be producing. Receive into your mind

the sweetness of my Spirit, He will flow into your soul and will wash away all earthly considerations.

10. The Son spoke, "How can a person recognise My Spirit, since there are two spirits, one good and one bad? I shall tell you, My Spirit is hot and has two effects. First, He makes one desire nothing but God; second, He grants utmost humility and contempt for the world. The bad spirit is both cold and hot, cold in that he makes bitter everything having to do with God, hot in that he inclines people to the lust of the flesh and worldly pride and rouses a desire for their own praise. He comes like a smooth-talking friend, but is really like a dog that bites. He comes like a soothing charmer, but is really the worst of ensnarers. When he comes, tell him, 'I do not want you, for your ends are evil.' When, however, the Holy Spirit comes, tell Him, 'Come like fire, Lord, and set my heart aflame! Though I am unworthy to receive You, yet for my part I need You. You will not be better because of me, nor do You need what I have, but I will become better through You and, without You, I am nothing.'"

GLORY BE TO THE FATHER   Glory be to the Father, and to the Son, and to the Holy Spirit, as it was in the beginning, is now and ever shall be, world without end. Amen.

THE FATIMA PRAYER   O my Jesus, forgive us our sins, save us from the fires of hell, lead all souls to heaven, especially those in most need of Thy mercy.

The Assumption of the Blessed Virgin

THE FRUIT OF THIS MYSTERY

A true and tender devotion to the Blessed Virgin

MY YOU RECEIVE ETERNAL honour and glory, O my Lady, O Virgin Mary,. When it pleased God to rescue you from the exile of this world and to honour your soul in His kingdom forever, He then deigned to announce this to you through His angel; and He willed that your venerable body, when dead, be entombed by His apostles in a sepulchre with all reverence.

OUR FATHER   Our Father, Who art in Heaven, hallowed be Thy name, Thy kingdom come, Thy will be done, on earth as it is in heaven. Give us this day our daily bread; and forgive us our trespasses, as we forgive those who trespass against us; and lead us not into temptation, but deliver us from evil. Amen.

HAIL MARY (10)   Hail Mary, Full of Grace, the Lord is with thee. Blessed art thou among women and blessed is the fruit of thy womb, Jesus. Holy Mary, Mother of God, pray for us sinners now, and at the hour of our death. Amen.

1. We may picture the Apostles and many holy ones around Mary as her last hour approached. We know the reverence and honour they paid to her at the moment of her death. We believe that she died, as all others die. We believe that her son, the Son of God, took her to Himself, and raised her, body and soul, to live for ever in heaven.

2. May you be blessed, my Lady, O Virgin Mary. In your ardent charity and maternal love, you unceasingly desired at every moment to come to your beloved son now sitting in heaven. While dwelling in this world and sighing after the things of heaven, you humbly conformed to the will of God; wherefore, by the dictates of divine justice, you ineffably increased your eternal glory.

3. St. Bridget said, "When I was in the Valley of Jehoshaphat, praying at the sepulchre of the glorious Virgin, that same Virgin appeared to me, shining with exceeding splendour, and said, "Be attentive, my daughter! After my son ascended to heaven, I lived in the world for fifteen years and as much

time more as there is from the feast of the Ascension of that same son of mine until my death. And then I lay dead in this sepulchre for fifteen days."

4. The Immaculate Virgin said, "Thereupon I was assumed into heaven with infinite honour and joy. The garments in which I was buried remained in the sepulchre and I was clothed in such garments as those that clothe my son and my Lord, Jesus Christ. Know also that there is no human body in heaven except the glorious body of my son and my own body."

5. The sinless body of Mary, together with her soul, was taken up by God after her death into heaven, and she is honoured there, body and soul, forever. No mind of ours can comprehend the perfection and glory which is Christ's as reward for His sufferings. No mind of ours can comprehend the glory which is Mary's, in body and soul, for her perfect obedience to God.

6. The bride of Christ exclaimed, "Elijah was so holy that he, with soul and body, was assumed into a holy earthly realm. But your soul, my most dear mother, was assumed above all the choirs of angels to the throne of God, along with your most pure body. You are therefore higher than Elijah and all the other saints."

7. Be glad, my Lady, O Virgin Mary. For in that most light death of yours, your soul was embraced by the power of God; and He, as a watchful father, protected it from all adversity. Then it was that God the Father subjected to your power all things created. With honour, God the Son placed you, His

most worthy mother, beside Himself on a most lofty seat. And the Holy Spirit, in bringing you to His glorious kingdom as a virgin betrothed to Himself, wonderfully exalted you.

8. Rejoice eternally, my Lady, O Virgin Mary. For some days after your death, your body lay entombed in its sepulchre until, with honour and through the power of God, it stood linked anew to your soul. Exult to the full, O Mother of God, O glorious Lady, O Virgin Mary. You merited to see your body revived after your death and assumed with your soul into heaven amidst honour from the angels. You acknowledged that your glorious son was God with a human nature; and with exultant joy, you saw that He is the most just judge of all and the rewarder of good works.

9. The Blessed Virgin said, "Afterwards, when my lifetime had been accomplished, my son first raised up my soul, for it was the mistress of the body, to a more excellent place than others in heaven, right next to His divinity. Later, He also raised up my body in such a manner that no other creature's body is so close to God as mine. See how much my son loved my soul and body! Yet, there are some people with a malevolent spirit who deny that I was assumed into Heaven, body and soul, and also others who simply do not know any better. But this is a most certain truth: I, with body and soul, was assumed to the Divinity!"

10. Who could measure the joy in heaven when God raised Mary from this earth? Who will measure our joy when, seeing God face to face, we see too the glory of Mary? The Angels rejoicing in Mary glorify God. The raising of Mary to heaven

has increased even the blessedness of heaven. To Adam and Eve, to the Patriarchs and Prophets, to all who died before Christ and were released by His death, to all who have died since Christ's death and been taken to heaven, Mary's entry into heaven is an everlasting joy and delight. They praise God for her glory, for the honour He has bestowed on her as the one who bore in holiness Christ, their Redeemer and Lord.

GLORY BE TO THE FATHER   Glory be to the Father, and to the Son, and to the Holy Spirit, as it was in the beginning, is now and ever shall be, world without end. Amen.

THE FATIMA PRAYER   O my Jesus, forgive us our sins, save us from the fires of hell, lead all souls to heaven, especially those in most need of Thy mercy.

The Coronation of the Blessed Virgin Mary and the Glory of all the Angels and Saints

THE FRUIT OF THIS MYSTERY

Personal submission to Our Lady as queen and mother

 " I AM THE QUEEN OF Heaven. You are concerned about how you should praise and honour me. Know and be certain that all praise of my son also is praise of me, and those who dishonour Him also dishonour me. This is so because I loved Him and He loved me so ardently that both of us were like one heart. He so magnificently honoured me, who was an earthen vessel, that He raised me above all the angels. Therefore, you should praise me like this, "May You be blessed O God, Creator of all things, Who deigned to descend into the womb of the Virgin Mary! May You be blessed, O God, Who went out of her without blemish, to the joy of her whole body! May You be blessed, O God, Who after your heavenly ascension gladdened the Virgin Mary, your Mother, with continuous comforts and visited her with your consolation! May You be blessed, O God, Who assumed the body and soul of the Virgin Mary, Your Mother, into heaven and honourably placed her above all the angels next to Your Divinity! Have mercy on me for the sake of her prayers!"

OUR FATHER   Our Father, Who art in Heaven, hallowed be Thy name, Thy kingdom come, Thy will be done, on earth as it is in heaven. Give us this day our daily bread; and forgive us our trespasses, as we forgive those who trespass against us; and lead us not into temptation, but deliver us from evil. Amen.

HAIL MARY (10)   Hail Mary, Full of Grace, the Lord is with thee. Blessed art thou among women and blessed is the fruit of thy womb, Jesus. Holy Mary, Mother of God, pray for us sinners now, and at the hour of our death. Amen.

1. Rejoice again, my Lady, O Virgin Mary. For your body's most holy flesh knows that it now exists in heaven as both virgin and mother. It sees itself in no way stained by any mortal or venial crime. No, it knows that it did all the works

of virtue with such charity that God, in justice, had to revere it with highest honour. Your flesh then understood that the more ardently that anyone loves God in this world, the nearer to Himself will God place that person in heaven. For it was manifestly clear to the whole court of heaven that no angel and no human loved God with such charity as you did; and therefore it was right and just that with honour God Himself placed you, body and soul, on the highest seat of glory.

2. We believe and we know, that Mary was assumed body and soul into heaven. We and all our race should ever think of her, and pray to her. In the trials and sorrows of our days, in the sinfulness of our hearts, in the bitterness of life, overshadowed by the certain approach of death. we should look to her, and draw near to her with true sorrow for sin.

3. The bride Christ, St Bridget, saw the Queen of Heaven, the Mother of God, wearing a priceless and beautiful crown on her head and her wonderfully shining and indescribably beautiful hair hanging down over her shoulders. She wore a golden tunic shining with an indescribable light, and a blue mantle of the colour azure or a clear sky. Full of wonder at such a lovely sight she stood there totally enraptured and amazed. At that moment, blessed John the Baptist appeared to her and said, "Listen closely to what all this signifies. The crown signifies that she is the Queen and Lady and Mother of the King of Angels; the hair hanging down signifies that she is an unstained and pure virgin; the sky coloured mantle signifies that all worldly things were as dead in her heart and will; the golden tunic signifies that she was fervent and burning in the love of God, both inwardly and outwardly."

4. Jesus Christ, her son, then placed seven lilies in her crown. The first lily is her humility; the second lily is her fear; the third, her obedience; the fourth, her patience; the fifth, her steadfastness; the sixth, her kindness, for she is kind and gives to all who beg of her with love and a will to amend; the seventh, her mercy in difficulties, for in whatever difficulty a man may be in, if he calls on her with all his heart, he will receive mercy and help from her because she is full of compassion and mercy.

5. Between these shining lilies the Son of God then placed seven precious gem stones. The first gem is her incomparable virtue, for there is no virtue in any other spirit or in any other body, which she does not have in a higher fashion. The second gem is her perfect purity, for the Queen of the kingdom of Heaven was so pure that from her first entrance into the world up to the final day of her death, not a single stain of sin was ever to be found in her; and none of all the devils could ever find enough impurity in her to fit on the head of a needle-point. The third gem was her beauty, for God is praised constantly by His saints for His mother's beauty, and all the holy angels and holy souls are filled with joy over her beauty. The fourth precious gem in the crown is the Virgin Mother's wisdom, for she is filled with all divine wisdom in God and all wisdom is fulfilled and perfected through her. The fifth gem is her power and might, for she is so powerful and strong with God in her that she can subdue anything that has been created. The sixth gem is her clarity, for she shines so clear that she even illuminates the angels, whose eyes are clearer than light, and the devils do not dare to look upon her clarity. The seventh gem is the fullness of every delight

and joy and all spiritual sweetness, for her fullness is such that there is no joy that she does not increase, no delight that is not made fuller and more perfect by her and through the blessed vision of her, for she is filled with grace and mercy above all the holy saints. All men must praise and honour the Virgin Mary, who is, in truth, so honoured and praised by her son.

6. St. Bridget revealed, "I saw the court of heaven preparing for judgement, and my ghostly ears and eyes were opened to hear and to see. And then I saw Abraham come with all the saints who were born of his generation. Then came all Patriarchs and Prophets. And afterwards I saw the four Evangelists, whose shape was like to four beasts, as they are painted upon walls in the world, except that they appeared to be living and not dead. After this, I saw twelve seats, and in them the twelve Apostles, waiting for the coming of the power. Then came Adam and Eve with Martyrs and Confessors and all other saints that came from them. But the manhood of Christ was not yet seen, nor the body of His Blessed Mother; but all waited for their arrival. The earth and the water seemed to be lifted up to Heaven, and all things that were in them humbled themselves, and with reverence bowed down. And then I heard the voice, crying out, 'O you, all heavens with all planets, be silent; and all you fiends who are in darkness, listen; and all you others that are in darkness, hear; for the sovereign emperor proposes to hear judgement upon the earth. There was also so great a multitude of holy souls, that my sight could not behold them in length, breadth, height and deepness. I saw also some places still empty, waiting to be filled to the worship of God. The Virgin who had come and sat by the Lamb said, 'O most sweet Lord, have mercy

upon sinners'. To her the Judge answered, 'It is not right to deny you anything. Therefore, those who cease from sin and do worthy penance shall find mercy; and judgement shall be turned away from them'"

7. The saint saw an unfathomably vast palace where there were countless figures dressed in white and shining clothes, each of whom seemed to have his or her own seat. In the principal part of the palace there was a judgment seat on which the sun seemed to sit. The rays that came from the sun were unfathomably long, deep, and wide. Next to this seat stood a maiden with a precious crown on her head, and all the servants of the sun that sat on the seat praised Him with hymns and songs. It was then explained to her, "My dear Lady Bridget, the palace you saw in the vision is an image of heaven. The great crowd of those who were seated and dressed in white and shining clothes are the angels and the souls of the saints. The sun signifies Christ in his divine nature; the woman stands for the Virgin who gave birth to God; the dark figure accusing the soul is the devil; the knight reporting the good works of the soul is an angel."

8. Will not the Son of God, being God, return good for good, and a five-fold reward even for a small act of charity? He promises in the Gospel that for every good work He will repay a hundredfold. Who can imagine then what will be Mary's reward? Her life was a life of countless good works, a life entirely pleasing to God, a life ever free from defect and unmarred by sin. In all things her will chose, and every member of her body responded gladly to that command. Each one of us however must also rise, body and soul. The

justice of God has willed that on the last day, each one of us will be repaid for our works.

9. The good works of Mary, accomplished by her perfect subjection of body to soul, proclaim for ever her praise. She has done all things as God willed, and omitted nothing that God desired, to win an eternal heavenly glory of both body and soul. No soul, except Christ's, was so filled with holiness and merit as the pure soul of Mary. No body, except the sacred body of her son, was so worthy to be glorified for its purity and perfection as the pure body of Mary. The holiness of Mary, those virtues adorning her soul, glorified God her Creator, and she is crowned now in heaven with His reward for those virtues.

10. May You be blessed, O my Lady, O Virgin Mary. Every faithful creature praises the Holy Trinity for you because you are the Trinity's most worthy creature. For wretched souls you obtain prompt pardon, and for all sinners you stand forth as a most faithful advocate and proxy. May God be praised, the most high Emperor and Lord, Who created you for such a great honour, that you should became both Empress and Lady, forever to reign with Him unto ages of ages.

GLORY BE TO THE FATHER   Glory be to the Father, and to the Son, and to the Holy Spirit, as it was in the beginning, is now and ever shall be, world without end. Amen.

THE FATIMA PRAYER   O my Jesus, forgive us our sins, save us from the fires of hell, lead all souls to heaven, especially those in most need of Thy mercy.

CONCLUDING PRAYERS   *Upon completing the recitation of the Holy Rosary, the following prayers are customary, but others too may be added according to one's devotion and preference.*

HAIL HOLY QUEEN   Hail Holy Queen, Mother of Mercy, hail our life, our sweetness and our hope. To thee do we cry, poor banished children of Eve, to thee do we send up our sighs, mourning and weeping in this vale of tears. Turn then, most gracious advocate, thine eyes of mercy towards us, and after this, our exile, show unto us the blessed fruit of thy womb, Jesus. O clement, O loving, O sweet Virgin Mary. Pray for us O holy Mother of God, that we may be made worthy of the promises of Christ.

Let Us Pray   O God, Whose only begotten son, by His life, death and resurrection, has purchased for us the rewards of eternal life, grant we beseech Thee, that meditating on these mysteries of the most Holy Rosary of the Blessed Virgin Mary, we may both imitate what they contain and obtain what they promise, through the same Christ our Lord. Amen.

PRAYER TO SAINT MICHAEL THE ARCHANGEL   Holy Michael, the Archangel, defend us in the day of battle. Be our safeguard against the wickedness and snares of the devil. May God rebuke him, we humbly pray; and do thou, O Prince of the heavenly hosts, by the power of God thrust down into hell Satan and all the evil spirits who wander through the world seeking the ruin of souls. Amen.

MEMORARE   Remember, O most gracious Virgin Mary, that never was it known that anyone who fled to thy protection, implored thy help, or sought thine intercession was left unaided. Inspired by this confidence, I fly unto thee, O Virgin of virgins, my mother; to thee do I come, before thee I stand, sinful and sorrowful. O Mother of the Word Incarnate, despise not my petitions, but in thy mercy hear and answer me. Amen.

May the Divine Assistance remain always with us, and may the souls of the faithful departed, through the mercy of God rest in peace. Amen.

The Mysteries of Light

The Baptism of Our Lord in the River Jordan

THE FRUIT OF THIS MYSTERY
Gratitude for the gift of Holy Baptism which begins the Life of Grace

THE LORD SAID, "AS to why I wanted to be baptised, I answer, anyone who wants to found or start a new way, must lead the way for others. The ancient people were given a way of the flesh, circumcision, as a sign of obedience and future purgation. Among the faithful observers of the law, this brought about a certain effect of future grace and a promise before the coming of the promised truth, that is, before I, the Son of God, came. With the coming of the truth, however, since the law was but a shadow, it had been eternally determined that the ancient way should fade and lose its effect. In order that the truth might appear, the shadow recede, and the way to heaven be more easily seen, I, God and man, born without sin, wished to be baptised as an example of humility for others and so that I might open up heaven for believers. As a sign of this, heaven was opened when I myself was baptised, and the voice of the Father was heard, and the Holy Spirit appeared in the likeness of a dove, and I, the Son of God, was revealed in My true humanity, so that all the faithful might know and believe that the Father opens heaven for the baptised faithful. When I, Who am Truth, came into the world, the shadow of the old covenant immediately disappeared, the shell of the law was broken, and the kernel appeared, circumcision ceased, and I Myself established baptism by means of which heaven is opened to young and old and the children of wrath become children of grace and eternal life.

OUR FATHER   Our Father, Who art in Heaven, hallowed be Thy name, Thy kingdom come, Thy will be done, on earth as it is in heaven. Give us this day our daily bread; and forgive us our trespasses, as we forgive those who trespass against us; and lead us not into temptation, but deliver us from evil. Amen.

HAIL MARY (10)   Hail Mary, Full of Grace, the Lord is with thee. Blessed art thou among women and blessed is the fruit of thy womb, Jesus. Holy Mary, Mother of God, pray for us sinners now, and at the hour of our death. Amen.

1. St. John the Baptist explained, "The Lord Jesus is the very Son of God by nature, He is the One of Whom I heard the Father bearing witness to when He said 'This is My Son'. From Him proceeds the Holy Spirit Who appeared above Him in the form of a dove as I was baptising Him. He is the son of the Virgin according to the flesh and I touched His body with my very own hands."

2. Then our Lord confirmed these things, saying, "It was the voice of God the Father that John the Baptist heard in the Jordan; It was My human body which John saw, touched and baptised; It was the Holy Spirit Who revealed Himself in the form of a dove."

3. The Eternal Word said, "One thing is the baptism of water, another that of blood, another that of wholehearted desire. I, Who know the hearts of all people, know how to take all of these circumstances into account. I am begotten without beginning, begotten eternally from the beginning. From the commencement I have known how to give individual persons the rewards they deserve and I give to each according as he deserves. Not the least little good done for the glory of God will go without its reward. This is why you should give many thanks to God that you were born of Christian parents in the age of salvation, for many people have longed to obtain and see that which is offered to Christians and yet have not obtained it."

4. The Mother of God appeared again and said to a servant of hers, "My child, you still have need of a horse and saddle. The spiritual signification of the horse is baptism. Just as a horse has its four legs and carries a man on the journey he must accomplish, so too baptism, as signified by the horse, carries a man in the sight of God and has four spiritual effects. The first effect is that the baptised are liberated from the devil and bound to the commandments and service of God. The second effect is that they are cleansed from original sin. The third is that they are made God's children and coheirs. The fourth is that heaven is opened to them."

5. "Yet how many there are today who, having reached the age of reason, pull the reins on the horse of baptism and ride it off on a false path! The baptismal path is true and rightly followed when people are instructed and upheld in good moral habits before reaching the age of reason and when, upon reaching the age of reason and carefully considering what was promised at the baptismal font, they keep their faith and love of God intact. However, they ride away from the right path and rein the horse in when they prefer the world and the flesh to God."

6. "The saddle of the horse, that is, of baptism, is the effect of the bitter passion and death of Jesus Christ, which gave baptism its efficacy. What is water if not an element? As soon as God's blood was poured out, God's word and the power of His outpoured blood entered into the element. Thus, by the word of God, the water of baptism became the means of reconciliation between humankind and God, the gate of mercy, the expulsion of demons, the way to heaven, and the

forgiveness of sins. So those who would boast of the power of baptism should first consider how the effect of baptism was instituted through bitter pain. We must all consider how bitter our redemption was, and how many times we have broken our baptismal vows, and what we deserve for relapses into sin."

7. When this was said, a horse suddenly appeared equipped with gilt ornaments. And the Mother said, "The horse's ornaments symbolise the gifts of the Holy Spirit that are given in baptism. No matter whether it is administered by a good or a bad minister, baptism takes away the ancestral offence, increases grace, pardons every sin, gives the Holy Spirit as a pledge, angels as guardians, and heaven as an inheritance. See, my child, these are the trappings of a spiritual knight. A knight who wears them will receive the ineffable wages with which he can purchase perpetual joy, most peaceful honour, eternal plenty and everlasting life."

8. God the Father explained to St. Bridget, "The baptismal water bears witness that you are the daughter of Christ's human nature through regeneration and the healing of original sin. The Father, Who is in the Son, bears witness that you belong to the Father and to the Son. The Holy Spirit, who is in the Father and the Son, the Spirit being in both, bears witness that, through true faith and love, you belong to the Three Persons and One God."

9. May You be blessed my Lord Jesus Christ. You willed that Your immaculate flesh be circumcised and that You be called Jesus. You willed to be offered by Your Mother in the temple. You had Yourself baptised in the Jordan by Your servant John.

For forty days, You wonderfully fasted in the desert. You permitted Yourself to be tempted by Your enemy, the devil, whom, when it so pleased You, You drove from Yourself with a single word. May You be blessed my Lord Jesus Christ.

10. Before I began to work My public ministry, a voice spoke out ahead of Me, saying, "The axe has been laid to the tree." This voice was none other than John the Baptist. He was sent before Me and cried out in the desert, "The axe has been laid to the tree," which is to say, "Let the human race be ready, for the axe is now ready, and it is time for me to prepare a way to the city to uproot every obstacle." When I came, I worked from sunrise to sunset, that is, I devoted myself to the salvation of humankind from the time of My incarnation until My death on the cross. At the start of My undertaking, I took flight into the wilderness away from My enemies, more precisely, from Herod who was pursuing Me; I was put to the test by the devil and suffered persecution from men. I made My way in the wilderness of this world and prepared a road through My blood and sweat. The world might well be called a wilderness, since it was lacking in every virtue and remained a wilderness of vice. It had only one road on which everyone was descending into hell, the damned toward damnation, the good towards darkness. I heard mercifully the longstanding desire for future salvation and came like a pilgrim in order to work. Unknown to them in My divinity and power, I prepared the road that leads to heaven. My friends saw this way and observed the difficulties of My work and the My eagerness of heart, and many of them followed Me into joy.

GLORY BE TO THE FATHER   Glory be to the Father, and to the Son, and to the Holy Spirit, as it was in the beginning, is now and ever shall be, world without end. Amen.

THE FATIMA PRAYER   O my Jesus, forgive us our sins, save us from the fires of hell, lead all souls to heaven, especially those in most need of Thy mercy.

The Miracle at the Wedding Feast of Cana

THE FRUIT OF THIS MYSTERY

A desire for intimacy with Christ, bridegroom of humanity, through His Holy Church

THE ALMIGHTY SAID, "I am the Creator of the heavens and the earth. I have three qualities, I am most mighty, most wise, and most virtuous. I am so mighty that all the angels in Heaven honour Me, the demons in hell dare not look upon Me, and all the elements obey My command. I am so wise that no one can fathom or understand My wisdom, and I have so great insight that I know all that has been and will come to be. Not the least little worm or any other animal, no matter how ugly it may seem, has been made without a cause. I am also so virtuous that all good flows from Me as from a good spring, and all sweetness emanates from Me as from a good wine. Therefore, no one can be mighty, wise, or virtuous without Me."

OUR FATHER   Our Father, Who art in Heaven, hallowed be Thy name, Thy kingdom come, Thy will be done, on earth as it is in heaven. Give us this day our daily bread; and forgive us our trespasses, as we forgive those who trespass against us; and lead us not into temptation, but deliver us from evil. Amen.

HAIL MARY (10)   Hail Mary, Full of Grace, the Lord is with thee. Blessed art thou among women and blessed is the fruit of thy womb, Jesus. Holy Mary, Mother of God, pray for us sinners now, and at the hour of our death. Amen.

1. When God My Father wanted to manifest His love at a point in time foreseen from eternity, He sent His wine, that is, He sent Me, His Son, into the nearest glass awaiting the coming of the wine, namely, into the womb of the Virgin, whose love for Me was more fervent than that of any other creature.

2. This Virgin loved Me and longed for Me so much that there was no hour in which she did not seek Me, yearning to become My handmaid. This is why she obtained the choicest

wine, and this has three qualities. First it has strength, because I emerged without the contact of a man; second, a most beautiful colour, for I came down in beauty from heaven on high ready to do battle; third, an excellent taste, intoxicating with the highest of blessings.

3. A saint praised the Blessed Virgin, saying, "You are truly mother and virgin and bride. The most beautiful wedding was celebrated in you at the time when a human nature was joined to God in you without any admixture or loss in His divinity. Virginity and motherhood were united while virginal modesty remained intact, and you became at the same time both mother and daughter of your Creator. This day you gave birth in time to Him who was eternally begotten of the Father and has wrought all things with the Father. The Holy Spirit, within and without you and all around you, made you fruitful as you gave your consent to God's herald. God's Son Himself, Who was born of you this day, was within you even before His herald came to you. Truly, God celebrated a wedding within you at the time of His incarnation."

4. The Lord said to St. Bridget, "I, the most powerful being of all, have compassion on their great misery and anguish. I acted like a rich and loving king who sent expensive wine to his intimate servants, saying, 'Pour it forth to many, for it is wholesome. It gives health to the sick, mirth to them who are depressed, and a courageous heart to those who are whole.' I have sent My words, which are like wine, to My servants by you, who are my vessel, which I will fill and draw out after My own will."

5. "To my servants I sent My words, which can be compared to the best of wine, and they shall give them to others, because My words are healthful. By the flask I mean you, who are hearing My words. You have done both things, for you have heard and delivered My words. You are My flask. I shall fill you whenever I like and drain you whenever I please. Thus, My Spirit will show you where you should go and what you should say. May you fear no one but Me. You must gladly go anywhere I wish and boldly say whatever I command you, for nothing can withstand Me. I will be there with you."

6. A person who is to be a light for others must consider what is fitting and proper before God, how to edify them, and what is profitable for their salvation. If bread and wine are missing from the material table, everything loses its taste. It is likewise at the spiritual table: Everything will be tasteless for the soul if the wine of spiritual joy and the bread of God's doctrine are missing. Thus, the father should say something to the glory of God while at table in order to strengthen spiritually those who are eating with him, or else he should see to it that something edifying is read, so that at one and the same bodily meal both the body may be refreshed and the soul may be instructed.

7. When a man comes to the dinner table, this should be his prayer, "O Lord Jesus Christ, You will that this corruptible body should be sustained with material food, I ask You to help me to give my body what it needs in such a way that it does not grow sluggish from too much food nor weak from too much frugality. Inspire in me a suitable moderation so that when this man of earth lives on the things of the earth,

the Lord of the earth may not be provoked to anger by his creature of earth." While at table, he may enjoy the company of those who are there with him, but above all, he must avoid saying anything that might confirm others in their vices or be an occasion of sin.

8. The Lord spoke to St. Bridget, "Therefore, I take you to Myself as My bride and for My own pleasure, the kind that is becoming for God to have with a chaste soul. It is the obligation of the bride to be ready when the bridegroom wants to celebrate the wedding so that she will be properly dressed and pure. You purify yourself well if your thoughts are always on your sins, on how I cleansed you in baptism from the sin of Adam, and how often I have been patient and supported you when you fell into sin. The bride should also have the insignia of her bridegroom on her chest, which means that you should observe and take heed of the favours and good deeds which I have done for you, such as how nobly I created you by giving you a soul and body, how nobly I enriched you by giving you health and temporal things, how lovingly and sweetly I redeemed you when I died for you and restored your heavenly inheritance to you, if you want to have it. The bride should also do the will of the Bridegroom. But what is my will, except that you should want to love Me above all things and not desire anything but Me? But if you, My bride, desire nothing but Me, if you despise all things for My sake, not only your children and relatives, but also honour and riches, I will give you the most precious and lovely reward! I will not give you gold or silver, but Myself, to be your Bridegroom and reward, I, Who am the King of Glory."

9. "My bride, you should be ready for the wedding of My Divinity wherein no fleshly lusts are found, but only the most sweet spiritual desire, the one that is becoming for God to have with a chaste soul. The love for your children, your friends, or your temporal belongings should not draw you away from My love. May it not happen to you what happened to those foolish virgins who were not ready when the Lord wanted to call them to the wedding and were therefore excluded."

10. The Lord explained, "Virginity is good and most excellent, for it resembles the angelic state, provided it is maintained with wisdom and virtue. But if the one is missing from the other, that is, if there is virginity of the flesh but not of the mind, then that virginity has been deformed. A devout and humble housewife is more acceptable to Me than a proud and immodest virgin. A God-fearing housewife, who is in control of herself and lives according to the rule of her state, can win equal merit as a humble and modest virgin. Although it is a great thing to stand the test of fire without burning, it is an equally great thing to remain outside the fire of the religious state but to be willing to be in the fire and to burn with greater ardour outside the fire than one does who is in the fire. I offer you the example of three women: Susanna, Judith, and Thecla the virgin. The first was married, the second a widow, the third a virgin. They had different ways of life and made different choices, but they gained a similar reward by their meritorious deeds. It is equally acceptable to Me whether your daughter remains a virgin or marries, provided that it is done according to My will. What would it profit her if she perhaps were cloistered in body but remained outside the walls in her mind? Or, which would be more glorious: to

live for herself or for the benefit of others? I know and foresee all things, and I do nothing without a reason."

GLORY BE TO THE FATHER   Glory be to the Father, and to the Son, and to the Holy Spirit, as it was in the beginning, is now and ever shall be, world without end. Amen.

THE FATIMA PRAYER   O my Jesus, forgive us our sins, save us from the fires of hell, lead all souls to heaven, especially those in most need of Thy mercy.

The Proclamation of the Kingdom and the Call to Conversion

HE SON SPOKE, "LET whoever so wishes read the scriptures, and they shall find that I made a prophet out of a shepherd and filled youths and simple people with the spirit of prophecy. It is true that not everyone has yet received My saving words, yet, in order to make My love known, My words have reached most people. Likewise, I did not choose scholars to preach the gospel but fishermen. In this way, they could not boast of their own wisdom. Thus, everyone would know that, just as God is wondrous and inconceivable, so too His works are inscrutable, and that He works the greatest miracles with the least of means.

OUR FATHER   Our Father, Who art in Heaven, hallowed be Thy name, Thy kingdom come, Thy will be done, on earth as it is in heaven. Give us this day our daily bread; and forgive us our trespasses, as we forgive those who trespass against us; and lead us not into temptation, but deliver us from evil. Amen.

HAIL MARY (10)   Hail Mary, Full of Grace, the Lord is with thee. Blessed art thou among women and blessed is the fruit of thy womb, Jesus. Holy Mary, Mother of God, pray for us sinners now, and at the hour of our death. Amen.

1. The Son explained, "There were two sisters, Martha and Mary, whose brother I raised from the dead. After his resurrection, he served Me more than before. His sisters, too, though they had been My servants and zealous in attending to Me before their brother's resurrection, showed themselves much more solicitous and devoted afterward. There were four reasons that moved Me to raise Lazarus. The first was that he had been My friend while he lived. The second was the love of his sisters. The third was that Mary's humility had earned such a reward when she washed My feet. She deserved to be gladdened and honoured to the extent to which she had lowered herself for My sake in the sight of the guests. The fourth reason was to manifest the glory of My human nature.

2. Then Christ spoke to His bride and said, "Tell My friends three things. When I was bodily in the world, I adjusted My words so that good men were made stronger and more fervent in doing good things, and evil men became better, as was seen in the conversion of Magdalene, Matthew, and many others. I also adjusted My words so that My enemies were not able to refute them. For that reason, may they to whom My words are sent, work with fervour, so that through My words, the good may become more ardent in goodness, the evil repent from wickedness, and that they themselves be on guard against My enemies so that My words are not obstructed. In truth, I do no greater injustice to the devil than to the angels in Heaven. For if I wanted, I could speak My words so that the whole world hears them. I could also open up hell so that everyone may see its torments, but this would not be justice, since all men would then serve Me out of fear, when they should serve me out of love. For no other than the one who has love shall enter the kingdom of Heaven. For I would be doing injustice to the devil if I took away from him one who is rightfully his, because of sin, and who is devoid of good deeds. I would also do injustice to the angel in Heaven, if I placed the spirit of an unclean man as an equal to the one who is pure and most fervent in My love.

3. That good man, Zacchaeus, and Mary Magdalene, insofar as they had offended God in all their limbs, gave Him all their limbs in reparation for their offences. Insofar as they had risen mortally in worldly rank, they lowered themselves humbly through the contempt of the world. Indeed, it is difficult to love God and the world at the same time. Zacchaeus and Magdalene converted and chose the better part."

4. The Son of God spoke, "I am like a ruler who fought faithfully in the land of his pilgrimage, and returned with joy to the land of his birth. This ruler had a very precious treasure. At its sight, the bleary-eyed became clear-sighted, the sad were consoled, the sick regained their strength, the dead were raised. For the purpose of the safe and honest protection of this treasure, a splendid and magnificent house of suitable height was built and finished with seven steps leading up to it and the treasure. The ruler entrusted the treasure to his servants for them to watch over, manage, and protect faithfully and purely. This was in order that the ruler's love for his servants might be shown and that the servants' faithfulness toward the ruler might be seen."

5. The Blessed Mother spoke, "There is a treasure I know of that whoever possesses it will never be poor, whoever sees it will never know distress and death, and whoever desires it will joyfully receive whatever he wishes. The treasure is my dearest son's precious words and the deeds He did during and before His passion, along with the miracles He worked when the Word was made flesh in my body and that He continues to do when, at God's word, the bread on the altar each day is changed into that same flesh. All these things are a precious treasure that has become so neglected and forgotten that there are very few people who recall it or draw any profit from it."

6. Sometimes God promises and miraculously grants bodily or carnal goods, but really He intends spiritual goods by them, so as both to spur the mind on in its fervour toward God by means of the gifts received and to keep it humble in its spiritual understanding so that it does not fall into presumption. That

is how God treated Israel. First He promised and gave them temporal goods, and also performed miracles for them, so that they might learn about invisible and spiritual goods by means of such things. Then, when their understanding had attained a better knowledge of God, He used obscure and difficult words to speak to them through the prophets, adding at times words of comfort and joy, as, for example, when He promised them a return to the fatherland, perpetual peace, and a restoration of all that was in ruins. Though the people were carnal minded, and understood and desired all these promises in a carnal way, still God in His foreknowledge decided beforehand that some promises would be fulfilled in a physical sense, but others spiritually.

7. The Lord lamented, "priests do not speak of My miracles or teach My doctrine but teach rather the love of the world. They preach their own pleasure and think nothing of what I did for them. Let all men sanctifying Me with their lips."

8. May you be blessed, O Lady Virgin Mary. You saw your son preaching, doing miracles, and choosing the apostles, who, being enlightened by His examples, His miracles, and His teachings, became witnesses of truth that your Jesus is truly the Son of God, publishing to all nations that it was He Who, through Himself, had fulfilled the writings of the prophets when on behalf of the human race He had patiently endured a most hard death.

9. May You be blessed, my Lord Jesus Christ. With Your blessed mouth, You preached to human beings the words of life; and in their sight, through Yourself, within Your actual

presence, You worked many miracles. May You be blessed, my Lord Jesus Christ. By fulfilling the writings of the prophets, You manifested to the world in a rational way that You are the true God.

10. Our Lady said, "When the faithless Pharisees saw the good works of my son, namely, the raising of the dead and the cleansing of leapers, they thought to themselves, 'This man does unheard of and extraordinary miracles. He overcomes anyone He wants with a word, He knows all our thoughts, and He does whatever He wants. If He is successful, we will all have to submit to His power and become His subjects.' Therefore, in order to avoid being subjected to Him, they crucified Him because of their envy. But many Christians are the same, for they see His great deeds and miracles everyday, and they take advantage of His good deeds and hear how they should serve Him and come to Him, but they think to themselves, 'If we must leave all our temporal belongings and follow His will and not our own, it will be heavy and unbearable.' They despise His will and refuse to freely submit to Him."

GLORY BE TO THE FATHER   Glory be to the Father, and to the Son, and to the Holy Spirit, as it was in the beginning, is now and ever shall be, world without end. Amen.

THE FATIMA PRAYER   O my Jesus, forgive us our sins, save us from the fires of hell, lead all souls to heaven, especially those in most need of Thy mercy.

The Transfiguration of the Lord on Mount Tabor

THE FRUIT OF THIS MYSTERY

A desire to remain with the Lord, to never leave His presence

HE LORD SAID, "YOU ask, then, why I did not show My divine nature openly as I did with My human nature. The reason is that My divine nature is spiritual but My human nature is bodily. Yet the divine and human natures are and were inseparable ever since they were first joined together. My divinity is uncreated, and all things that exist are made in it and through it, and every perfection and beauty is found in it. If such beauty and perfection were visibly revealed to eyes of clay, who would be able to bear the sight? Who could look upon the physical sun in all its brightness? Who would not be terrified by the sight of lightning and the sound of thunder? How much greater the terror would be if the Lord of lightning and the Creator of all things were seen in His splendour!"

OUR FATHER   Our Father, Who art in Heaven, hallowed be Thy name, Thy kingdom come, Thy will be done, on earth as it is in heaven. Give us this day our daily bread; and forgive us our trespasses, as we forgive those who trespass against us; and lead us not into temptation, but deliver us from evil. Amen.

HAIL MARY (10)   Hail Mary, Full of Grace, the Lord is with thee. Blessed art thou among women and blessed is the fruit of thy womb, Jesus. Holy Mary, Mother of God, pray for us sinners now, and at the hour of our death. Amen.

1. The kind of wisdom that leads to a blessed life involves a rocky approach and a steep climb, inasmuch as resisting your passions seems a hard and rocky way. It involves a steep climb to spurn habitual pleasures and not to love worldly honours. Although it is difficult, yet for the person who reflects on how little time there is and how the world will end and who fixes his mind constantly on God, above the mountain there will appear a cloud, that is, the consolation of the Holy Spirit. Such consolation seems dark to the lovers of this world, for

they love darkness. But to the lovers of God it is brighter than the sun and shines more than gold.

2. The Lord said to the prophet and patriarch, "I ask you, Who brought you out of slavery into freedom? Who divided the waters for you? Who gave you the Law? Who gave you the prophetic spirit to speak about future things?" They answered Him, saying, "You, Lord. You brought us out of slavery. You gave us the Law. You moved our spirit to speak and prophesy about future things."

3. The Lord said, "I am the God Who in ancient days was called the God of Abraham, the God of Isaac and the God of Jacob. I am the God Who gave the Law to Moses. This law was like clothing. For as a mother with her child in the womb prepares her infant's clothing, so too I, God, prepared the New Law, for the Old Law was nothing but the clothing and shadow and sign of future things to come. I clothed and wrapped Myself in the clothing of this Law. And then, when a boy grows up, his old clothes are laid down and new clothes are taken up. In this way, I fulfilled the Old Law when I put aside the used clothing of the Old Law, and assumed the new clothing, that is, the New Law."

4. The Lord explained, "My divinity was not openly revealed for two reasons. The first reason is the weakness of the human body, whose substance is earthly. If any human body were to see the divinity, it would melt like wax before fire, and the soul would rejoice with such exultation that the body would be reduced, as it were, to ashes. The second reason is that If I were to show bodily eyes My divinity, which is incomparably

more radiant than fire and sun, I would be contradicting Myself. For I have said, 'No one shall see Me and live.' Not even the prophets themselves saw Me as I am in My divine nature. Those who did hear the voice of My divinity and saw the burning mountain were terrified and said, 'Let Moses speak to us, and we shall listen to him.'"

5. "I, the merciful God, in order to be understandable to humankind, revealed Myself to them in a human form like theirs, which they could see and touch and in which the divine nature is concealed, so that people might not be terrified by a form unlike their own. Insofar as I am God, I am not bodily and cannot be portrayed in a bodily manner, but people can endure to see and hear Me in My human nature."

6. The Virgin Mary said to St. Bridget, the bride of Christ, "My son's bride, love my son, for He loves you, and honour His saints who stand in His presence, for they are like countless stars whose light and brilliance cannot be compared to any worldly light. Just like the light of the world differs from darkness, yet even more does the light of the saints differ from the light of this world. In truth, I tell you that if the saints were seen in their brightness as they really are, no human eye could set eyes on them or endure it without losing their sight and life."

7. A holy man is ardent in his love of God, indeed, he becomes like a fire, warming those who have grown cold and overtaking the wicked. Sinners are unworthy to see this light, blinded as they are by their own love. They are unable to perceive this light, for their eyes are sick with pride. People with scabby

hands cannot touch this light. This light is hateful to the greedy and to those who love their own will.

8. Those who truly love God do not allow any of His rivals to enter the soul, to climb over any of its walls. Indeed, just as one who is inside a house is always surrounded by walls wherever one turns, so it is with the person who, day and night, with supreme longing, desires to see God in His glory and to praise Him with His holy angels. Truly, wherever such a one turns or whatever work he is intent upon, he is then always preserved unharmed inside firm walls so that, as a result, by dwelling among the very angels in this life, he may be said to enjoy the company of God.

9. Our Lady explained, "In the dwelling places that belongs to the friends of my son, the door is always completely open for to Him. They are glad to hear Him calling. They not only open when he knocks but joyfully run to meet Him as He comes in. They prepare a resting-place for my son, not out of the feathers of birds but out of the harmony of the virtues and the curbing of evil affections, which is the very marrow of all the virtues. They offer my son a kind of warmth that does not come from wool but from a love so fervent that they not only give their belongings to Him but their very selves as well. They also prepare food for Him that is fresher than any meat: it is their perfect heart that does not desire or love anything but that God, The Lord of Heaven, dwells in their hearts, and God Who nourishes all things is sweetly nourished by their charity. They keep their eyes continually on the door lest the enemy enter, they keep their ears turned

toward the Lord, and their hands ready for doing battle against the enemy. Imitate them as far as you are able."

10. The Lord said to the apostles, "Who was it that you saw, heard, and touched?" They answered, "We heard Your words and wrote them down. We heard and saw the great works that You did when You gave us the New Law. You commanded the demons with one word to leave humans and they obeyed You and went out, and with Your word You raised the dead and healed the sick. We saw You in a human body. We saw Your great power and divine glory with Your human nature. We touched Your hair and Your face, You ate with us and You gave us Your eloquence. You are truly the Son of God and the Son of the Virgin."

GLORY BE TO THE FATHER   Glory be to the Father, and to the Son, and to the Holy Spirit, as it was in the beginning, is now and ever shall be, world without end. Amen.

THE FATIMA PRAYER   O my Jesus, forgive us our sins, save us from the fires of hell, lead all souls to heaven, especially those in most need of Thy mercy.

The Institution of the Holy Eucharist

THE FRUIT OF THIS MYSTERY

A spirit of reparation for sins committed against the Blessed Sacrament, especially by priests

HE SON OF GOD said, "I am that bread that is seen and touched on the altar and is transformed into My body that was crucified. For just as a dry and easily inflammable piece of wood is quickly consumed if it is placed on the fire, and nothing remains of the wood but all of it is fire, so when these words are said, 'This is My body,'

that which before was bread instantly becomes My body, but is not inflamed by fire like wood but by My Divinity."

OUR FATHER   Our Father, Who art in Heaven, hallowed be Thy name, Thy kingdom come, Thy will be done, on earth as it is in heaven. Give us this day our daily bread; and forgive us our trespasses, as we forgive those who trespass against us; and lead us not into temptation, but deliver us from evil. Amen.

HAIL MARY (10)   Hail Mary, Full of Grace, the Lord is with thee. Blessed art thou among women and blessed is the fruit of thy womb, Jesus. Holy Mary, Mother of God, pray for us sinners now, and at the hour of our death. Amen.

1. May You be blessed, my Lord Jesus Christ. You foretold Your death ahead of time. At the last supper, from material bread You wonderfully consecrated Your precious Body and charitably bestowed it on Your apostles in memory of Your most worthy passion. By washing their feet with Your own precious and holy hands, You humbly showed Your very great humility.

2. The Lord said, "I was like a man about to depart from this world who entrusts his greatest possessions to his dearest friends. When I was about to depart from this world, I accordingly entrusted the thing dearest to Me, My own body, to priests whom I chose to be above all the angels and above all other men. Now, however, they treat Me just as the Jews did who denied that I had raised Lazarus and performed other miracles, and who instead spread the rumour that I wanted to be made king, that I had prohibited paying the tribute tax,

and that I would rebuild the temple in three days. See, My friends, what sort of priests I have! See, My angels, the ones whom you serve! If I lay before you as I lie on the altar before them, none of you would dare to touch Me. You would be afraid to do so. These men, however, betray Me like thieves and traitors. Like an unfaithful spouse they touch Me. They are filthier than tar, yet they do not feel ashamed to approach Me, Who am the God and Lord of glory. Accordingly, as it was said to Israel, 'seven plagues shall come upon you.' Those seven plagues shall surely come upon those priests who betray Me!"

3. "Three good things come from the offering of any of My priests. First, My patience is praised by all the heavenly host because I remain the same in the hands of good as well as of bad priests, and because there is no partiality in Me, and because this sacrament is brought about not by human merits but by My words. Second, this offering benefits everybody, no matter which priest offers it. Third, it benefits those who offer it as well, however bad they may be. Just as the single phrase 'I am' made My enemies collapse physically on the ground, so too when My words 'This is my body' are spoken, the devils flee from tempting the souls of the ministers, and they would not dare to return to them with such audacity, if the desire to sin was not there. I tell you truly, My daughter, it is a great thing to be called a priest. An angel of the Lord is also a mediator, but the priest's office is greater, for he touches the unfathomable God, and in his hands the lowest things are joined to the things of heaven."

4. "Just as I showed Myself in a different shape to the disciples on the way to Emmaus, and though I was true God and

true man when I came to the disciples through locked doors, so too I show myself beneath a different shape by means of priests so that faith may have its reward and human ingratitude may be revealed. That is no wonder, I am still the same now as when I revealed the power of My divinity by means of fearful signs and portents, and yet the people said at the time, "Let us make gods who can precede us." I also revealed My humanity to the Jews, and they crucified it. I am the same each day on the altar, and they say, 'We are disgusted and solely tried by this food'. What greater ingratitude can there be than to try to comprehend God with one's reason and dare to judge the secret counsels and mysteries in God's own power and possession? Hence, by means of an invisible effect and a visible form, I wish to reveal to the unlearned and humble what the visible form of bread is without the substance of bread. It is in order that the humble may be exalted and the proud be put to shame that I endure such indignities and outrages upon My body."

5. The saint spoke of a time of great sacrilege against the blessed sacrament, "O Rome, if you knew your days, you would surely weep and not rejoice. Rome was in olden days like a tapestry dyed in beautiful colours and woven with noble threads. Its soil was dyed in red, that is, in the blood of martyrs, and woven, that is, mixed with the bones of the saints. Now her gates are abandoned, in that their defenders and guardians have turned to avarice. Her walls are thrown down and left unguarded, in that no one cares that souls are being lost. The sacred vessels are sold with scorn, in that God's sacraments are administered for money and worldly favours. The altars are abandoned, in that the priest who celebrates

with the vessels has hands empty as to love for God but keeps his eyes on the collection; although he has God in his hands, his heart is empty of God, for it is full of the vain things of the world. The holy of holies, where the highest sacrifice used to be consumed, represents the desire to see and enjoy God. From this desire, there should rise up love for God and neighbour and the fragrance of temperance and virtue. However, the sacrifice is now consumed in the portico, that is, in the world, in that the love for God has completely turned into worldly vanity and lack of temperance. Such is Rome; many altars are abandoned, the collection is spent in taverns, and the people who give to it have more time for the world than for God. Yet Rome is still not without friends of God. If they were given some help, they would cry out to the Lord and He would have mercy on them."

6. A monstrous creature appeared to the bride at the elevation of the body of Christ and said, "Do you really believe, silly woman, that this wafer of bread is God? None of the wise Jews to whom God has given wisdom believes this, nor can anyone believe that God would allow Himself to be touched and loved by a most impure priest with the heart of a dog." Right then, a good angel appeared and said, "O, daughter, answer not a fool according to his folly! It is the father of lies who has appeared to you. But get ready, for our bridegroom is now near." Jesus the Bridegroom came and said to the devil, "Why are you troubling My daughter and bride? I call her daughter, because I created her, and I call her bride, because I redeemed her and have joined her to Myself through My love." Then the Lord said to the bride, "This is what is now taking place on the altar. Prior to the sacramental words, the

bread on the altar is bread. When the words 'This is My body' are spoken, the bread becomes the body of Christ that people receive, both the good and the wicked, one person as much as one thousand, according to the same truth but not with the same effect, for the good receive it unto life, while the wicked receive it unto judgment. What the devil said about God being defiled by the impurity of the offering minister is most truly false. Just as a sick person is able offer medicinal mixtures made from potent herbs, accordingly, God is not made bad because of the badness of a bad minister nor better because of a good minister, for God is always unchangeable and always the same.

7. The tree of life is Mary, the sweet fruit of this tree, Christ her Son. We reach through the branches to pluck the fruit when we greet Mary, as Gabriel did, with great love. She offers us her sweet fruit to taste when she sees our hearts no longer in sin, but willing in all things the will of God. Her intercession and prayer help us to receive the most holy Body of Christ, consecrated for us by the hands of men. This is the Food of true Life, the bread of Angels, and the nourishment of sinful men. With wise thoughts, therefore, and with care, with all reverence and love, take Him and eat.

8. St. Bridget revealed, "When the court of heaven was laid open to me, I saw an altar that was in the seat of the majesty, and a chalice with wine and water, and bread in the likeness of a host offered up upon the altar. Then, at the same time I saw how in a church on earth a priest began to offer mass, arrayed in his vestments. And when he had done all that belonged to the Mass, and came to the words with which

he should bless the host, I saw the sun, the moon, the stars and all the other planets moving in their course around this place. All the heavens sounded with the sweetest note and a song and melody was heard that stood beyond any human speech or comprehension. Those who were in the light beheld the priest and bowed themselves to the power with reverence and worship, and those who were in darkness shuddered and were afraid. When the words of God were said by the priest upon the host, it seemed to me that the same sacred host was in the seat of the majesty, staying nevertheless in the hands of the priest. And the same holy host was made as a living Lamb, and in the Lamb appeared the face of Our Lord. And a burning flame was seen within and without the sacred host. All the angels were present, as great a multitude as the beams of the sun. And a marvellous shining proceeded from the Lamb."

9. Our Lady said, "The human nature of Christ, which He drew from me, is the most precious created thing there ever was or is. Accordingly, when the righteous soul receives God's body with love and when His body fills the soul, the most precious thing there ever was is there, God's human nature, that has the divine nature within and without it. God is in him and he in God, just as God is in me and I in Him. As my servant and I share one God, in Holy Communion we share one bond of love and one Holy Spirit, Who is one God, with the Father and the Son."

10. St. Bridget praised the Blessed Virgin, saying, "The Son of God, though He is truly the food of Angels, could not be our food without that flesh and blood which He took from

your loving womb. Wine cannot refresh us unless it is in something we can drink from. The Holy Spirit could not be poured out upon us without the humanity of your son. For you, Virgin Mary, God Himself was to be your eternal meal, Father, Son and Holy Spirit, Three yet One. And through you He was to give Himself to men as the food of life. So, in a way, we may attribute this food of life to you, Mary, since it is by you that it has come to us. Just as wheat is made into flour, and then bread, for our daily use, so the Bread of Life came to us through you. The love of God the Father could not be made known on earth without the humanity of the Son, that humanity which He took from you, His Virgin Mother."

GLORY BE TO THE FATHER   Glory be to the Father, and to the Son, and to the Holy Spirit, as it was in the beginning, is now and ever shall be, world without end. Amen.

THE FATIMA PRAYER   O my Jesus, forgive us our sins, save us from the fires of hell, lead all souls to heaven, especially those in most need of Thy mercy.

CONCLUDING PRAYERS   *Upon completing the recitation of the Holy Rosary, the following prayers are customary, but others too may be added according to one's devotion and preference.*

HAIL HOLY QUEEN   Hail Holy Queen, Mother of Mercy, hail our life, our sweetness and our hope. To thee do we cry, poor banished children of Eve, to thee do we send up our sighs, mourning and weeping in this vale of tears. Turn then, most gracious advocate, thine eyes of mercy towards us, and after this, our exile, show unto us the blessed fruit of thy womb,

Jesus. O clement, O loving, O sweet Virgin Mary. Pray for us O holy Mother of God, that we may be made worthy of the promises of Christ.

Let Us Pray O God, Whose only begotten son, by His life, death and resurrection, has purchased for us the rewards of eternal life, grant we beseech Thee, that meditating on these mysteries of the most Holy Rosary of the Blessed Virgin Mary, we may both imitate what they contain and obtain what they promise, through the same Christ our Lord. Amen.

PRAYER TO SAINT MICHAEL THE ARCHANGEL Holy Michael, the Archangel, defend us in the day of battle. Be our safeguard against the wickedness and snares of the devil. May God rebuke him, we humbly pray; and do thou, O Prince of the heavenly hosts, by the power of God thrust down into hell Satan and all the evil spirits who wander through the world seeking the ruin of souls. Amen.

MEMORARE Remember, O most gracious Virgin Mary, that never was it known that anyone who fled to thy protection, implored thy help, or sought thine intercession was left unaided. Inspired by this confidence, I fly unto thee, O Virgin of virgins, my mother; to thee do I come, before thee I stand, sinful and sorrowful. O Mother of the Word Incarnate, despise not my petitions, but in thy mercy hear and answer me. Amen.

May the Divine Assistance remain always with us, and may the souls of the faithful departed, through the mercy of God rest in peace. Amen.

The Hopeful Mysteries

The Creation of all things in Christ

FRUIT OF THIS MYSTERY

Awe of God's plan, decreed from eternity

ADAM AND EVE OWED their beginning in some way to a special creation by God. Even this would not be fitting for the coming of God to earth. It would seem that Adam understood from God's words something of what was to be. At least, we may picture him foreseeing the future, foreseeing a woman, like Eve in womanhood, but lovelier and holier than all of his race, a virgin and mother,

149

bringing God Himself to this world. So we may think of Adam rejoicing with great joy at the thought, Mary, of your coming, as we know the Angels rejoiced, before the creation of the world, foreseeing your creation by God.

OUR FATHER   Our Father, Who art in Heaven, hallowed be Thy name, Thy kingdom come, Thy will be done, on earth as it is in heaven. Give us this day our daily bread; and forgive us our trespasses, as we forgive those who trespass against us; and lead us not into temptation, but deliver us from evil. Amen.

HAIL MARY (10)   Hail Mary, Full of Grace, the Lord is with thee. Blessed art thou among women and blessed is the fruit of thy womb, Jesus. Holy Mary, Mother of God, pray for us sinners now, and at the hour of our death. Amen.

1. God is the Creator of all beings, and He is Being itself. Nothing can be or come to be without God. Therefore, this world and all things in it owe their existence to Him alone. He is the Creator of all. And Creator, last of all, of man. To mankind He gave, as He had given to the Angels, the gift of free will. He wished that be free choice man would cling to what was good, and so avoid a just punishment and earn a just reward. God created man, forming him from the dust of the earth. He looked for man's love and obedient service, that so the places of those Angels who had disobeyed in their pride, and fallen from joy into misery, might be filled once more. They should have received a crown of joy for their love and obedience.

2. It was love that led God to create. There could be nothing lacking in God, nothing wanting to His goodness or his joy. It was out of love alone that He willed creation, that there might be beings, apart from Himself, who would partake of His infinite goodness and joy. So the Angels came to be, created by God in countless numbers. To them He gave free will, freedom to act, in accordance with their nature, as they willed. As He himself is under no necessity but has created out of love alone, He wills that the Angels, whom He designed for eternal happiness with Him, should likewise be under no necessity. He looked for love in response to His love, obedience to His offer of eternal joy. Yet in the first moment of their creation, there were Angels who chose, freely and deliberately against their Creator, in spite of His infinite love, which called them to love in return. Justly they fell, fixed in their evil will, from an eternal joy into an eternal misery. But not all fell. To those Angels who chose love for love, there was given the contemplation of God in all His glory, power and holiness From this contemplation, they came to know the eternity of God, that He has no beginning and no end; they learnt what it meant to have Him for their Creator; and they saw most clearly how everything they possessed had come to them from His love and His power. They learnt too that His wisdom had given them a wisdom of their own, but which He allowed them to foresee the future. And it was a joy and consolation to them to know that God in His mercy and love wished to replace, in His own way, those Angels who had forfeited by pride and envy their place in heaven.

3. In their contemplation of God, the angels saw with wonder a throne placed next to that of God Himself. They knew that

the one for whom this throne had been prepared had not yet been created. Yet already they loved this chosen one, and rejoiced as they waited. Their love for each other was born of their love for God. But between these two loves they saw one who was more lovable than themselves, one whom God loves with great joy more than all His creatures. Virgin Mary, you were the chosen one, destined for that throne near to the throne of God.

4. It was you, O Virgin, whom the angels loved, after God, from the first moment of their creation, seeing in the contemplation of God, how beautiful He had made themselves, but how much more beautiful He would make you. They saw that in you there would be a love and a joy far greater than their own. They saw too the crown that awaited you, a crown of glory and beauty surpassed only by the majesty of God. They knew how God their Creator was glorified by themselves and they rejoiced. They knew how much more He would be glorified by you, and they rejoiced still more. Before ever you were created, Mary, Almighty God and His angels together rejoiced in you.

5. The angelic host was seen standing before God, and the entire host said, "May You be praised and honored Lord God, Who are and were without end! We are Your servants and we praise and honor You for a threefold reason, first, because You created us to rejoice with You and gave us an indescribable light in which to rejoice forever. Second, because all things are created and maintained by Your goodness and constancy, and all things stand according to Your will and remain through Your word. Third, because You created mankind and took

manhood for their sake! We rejoice greatly for this manhood, and also for Your most chaste mother who was worthy to bear You, Whom the heavens cannot comprehend and enclose."

6. God's creation of the world and all it contains took place in the instant of His will's expression, and with the design and perfection foreseen by Him. Yet there remained still uncreated another work of creation which would surpass what He had already done. You, Mary, are, as it were, another world, a world which God foresaw with greater joy, a world the Angels were more pleased to contemplate, a world of more benefit to those of good will that the whole earth and all it contains. Mary, we see in God's act of creation and in all created things an image of your creating. We read that it pleased God to separate the darkness from the light when he created the earth. How much more it pleased Him to enlighten you from childhood. The darkness, the time of your infancy, was made light by your knowledge of God, your understanding of God, and the will to love God which day by day led you on to a love surpassed only by God Himself. The mental darkness of childhood, without knowledge of God, without reasoning power to guide, is for us a time of defencelessness and danger. But we know that for you, exempt from sin, it was a time of purest innocence.

7. We read that it pleased God to make, together with the stars, two lights, the sun for daytime, the moon for the night. It pleased God still more, Mary, to set in you two heavenly lights, brighter and more beautiful than the sun or the moon: the first, perfect obedience, a radiant light for Angels and men to admire, guiding all who saw it to God Himself, Who is the

light of eternal day; the second, a most complete and trusting faith, the light to men in the darkness of despair and unbelief when your son chose suffering and death, a light to cast out all shadow of doubt and uncertainty when He rose from the dead. We read that it pleased God to create the stars. The thoughts of your heart, Mary, were more pleasing to Him.

8. We read that it pleased God to create the birds, whose flight and song are a delight to men. All the words which you spoke, Mary, heard also in heaven to the joy of the Angels, were more pleasing still. We read that God created the earth itself, the dry land and the soul; and flowering and fruit-bearing trees of many kinds. Your life, Mary, your occupations and work, were more pleasing to Him, for you would give nourishment, and life itself, to all, and your love would make each act of your life more beautiful to God and the Angels than the fairest of flowers are to men. God created the plants, flowers, trees, and fruits, minerals, metals, and precious stones, He has made the earth rich with these things. Yet He saw in you, Mary, even before your creating, more qualities and virtues than in all earthly things.

9. We read that God's creation was pleasing to Him, and that He looked with joy on all He had done. It pleased Him still more to create you, Mary, and He looked with greater joy on you, even before your creating, than on this earth and all earthly things. That world and everything in it, all would be destroyed. Though created before you, Mary, it would not endure. But you, by God's eternal decree, were created to be for ever, and to be for ever united to Him in deepest love,

created in fullest grace, responding to His grace in all things, and so growing to the perfection of holiness.

10. Mary, we know that you were ever in the mind of God, before His creating brought you to be, the most perfect of all His creatures. He knew you, just as Noah knew the Ark he was to build and the way he was to build it, even before the flood came. The design of the Ark had been made known to Noah, and he waited for the time when God would command him to set to work. The design and perfection, Mary, of your glorious body, the Ark of God, was known to God before all time. And He knew the time when He would bring it into being by His creating. As Noah rejoiced at the thought of the Ark he was to build, so God rejoiced, Mary, at the thought of you. Noah's Ark would withstand the storms; you, Mary, the Ark of God, would withstand, in the strength of your holiness, every attack of the hatred and sin of hell.

GLORY BE TO THE FATHER   Glory be to the Father, and to the Son, and to the Holy Spirit, as it was in the beginning, is now and ever shall be, world without end. Amen.

THE FATIMA PRAYER   O my Jesus, forgive us our sins, save us from the fires of hell, lead all souls to heaven, especially those in most need of Thy mercy.

The Promise of the Redeemer and Co-Redemptrix

THE FRUIT OF THIS MYSTERY

Gratitude to God for His ineffable patience with humanity

WE MAY THINK OF Adam grieving at the words spoken to Eve by the Devil. But rejoicing, his sorrow turning to joy, at the thought of Mary. We may think of Adam grieving that Eve his wife, created by God from his body, had deceived him and drawn him on to eternal death.

But rejoicing that the Virgin Mary would bear in all purity Christ, the Son of God, to restore man to life. Grieving that Eve's first act was of disobedience; rejoicing that Mary would be a daughter of God, most dear to Him in all things, ever obedient to His will. Grieving that Eve had been tempted, in the sight of God and all the Angels, by the false promise of being made like to God; rejoicing that in the sight of God and the Angels, Mary, would acknowledge herself the Handmaid of God. Grieving that Eve had offended God, and brought about the condemnation of man; rejoicing that the Virgin's word to God should bring such joy to to all men. Grieving that Eve had closed to man the gate of heaven; rejoicing that Mary's word would open that gate again to himself and to all who sought to enter.

OUR FATHER   Our Father, Who art in Heaven, hallowed be Thy name, Thy kingdom come, Thy will be done, on earth as it is in heaven. Give us this day our daily bread; and forgive us our trespasses, as we forgive those who trespass against us; and lead us not into temptation, but deliver us from evil. Amen.

HAIL MARY (10)   Hail Mary, Full of Grace, the Lord is with thee. Blessed art thou among women and blessed is the fruit of thy womb, Jesus. Holy Mary, Mother of God, pray for us sinners now, and at the hour of our death. Amen.

1. In time, like the mountain streams which join, and then join to other streams as they descend, increasing ever in volume and power, carrying all before them, down at last to meet other waters and in the lower lands form into the great rivers, the Holy Spirit filled the hearts of His Prophets,

and first one, then another, then more raised their voices, to speak as He inspired them, till their sound filled the ears of many, to comfort and console, to call back and restore. The sweetest sound of their voices was that news of joy, that God Himself would be born of a Virgin, to make amends for the evil which Satan, through Adam, had caused to man; that He would redeem man, and rescue him from his misery, restoring to him eternal life.

2. Consenting to the suggestion of the enemy, Eve sinned, saying, "Let us eat of the Tree of Life, and we shall know all things, good and evil". And they fell, but not as did the Enemy; for the Evil One had true envy of God, and his wretchedness shall never end. Although Adam and Eve disobeyed God, they suffered justice with mercy. They felt justice insofar as they had nakedness in exchange for the clothing of glory, hunger for plenty, dread for security, and labour for rest. But soon they obtained mercy; that is to say, clothing against nakedness, food against hunger, security through coming together for the increasing of mankind.

3. The Prophets knew that the Son of God would come into the world, to be light in our darkness, brighter than the sun at dawn, to proclaim God's justice and love. But they knew He would not come unheralded. As the morning star heralds the sun, they foresaw that a star would rise in Israel, fairest of all the stars, in brightness and beauty surpassed only by the sun itself. This star with the Virgin Mary, who would be Mother of Christ, her love surpassed only by the love of God, her heart ever responding to the will of God.

4. This news was given by God to His Prophets, to console them in their labour of teaching, and encourage them in their trials. For they grieved at the pride and sinfulness of the people, who neglected the Law of Moses, rejected God's love, and incurred His anger. But they rejoiced, Mary, in you, foreseeing that God, that giver of all law, would receive back to His grace those who had sinned, for the sake of your humility and holiness of life. They grieved to see the temple empty and desolate, and the worship of God neglected. They rejoiced, Mary, to foresee the creation of that holy temple, your pure body, where God Himself would love to reside. They grieved at the destruction of the gates and the walls of the holy city, broken by armies, invaded by sin. They rejoiced, Mary, to foresee how you would stand firm, against all attack, a strong citadel where Christ would arm Himself, the gate through which He would come forth to His conflict with the Devil and his own. To the prophets, as to the patriarchs, your coming, Mary, was a thing of wonder and joy.

5. All humans have been given both good angels for their protection, and bad angels to test them. The good angels are not separated from God; they serve the soul without leaving God. They are constantly in His sight. Yet they work to inflame and incite the soul to do good. All the demons, however, shudder with fear at the name of Mary! When they hear the name, "Mary", they immediately release a soul out of the claws with which they had held her. Just as a bird or hawk, with its claws and beak embedded into its prey, releases it immediately if it hears a sound, but soon returns when it sees that no action follows, so do the demons, frightened when they hear that

holy name, release the soul. But they return and fly back as fast as an arrow if no improvement follows.

6. Adam's punishment made him see the justice and mercy of God. Throughout his life he feared to offend God and was guided in all things by love for God. This way of life he handed on to those who came after him. With time they forgot God's justice and mercy. They believed only what pleased them, immersing themselves in pleasure and sin. So came the flood, when God destroyed all men on earth, saving only Noah and those with him in the Ark, through whom He willed to people the earth again. Once again men multiplied on the earth, and once again they fell, tempted away from God, turning to the worship of false gods and idols. God's mercy and fatherly love led Him to intervene, and He chose one who was a faithful follower of His law, Abraham, to make a covenant with him and his descendants. He fulfilled his desire for a son, and Isaac was born. And He promised that from his descendants, Christ, His son, would come. It is possible that Abraham, by God's permission, foresaw many things. We may think of him as having foreseen Mary, the Mother of Christ. We may think of him rejoicing in her, and loving her more than Isaac his son.

7. It was not greed or ambition that led Abraham to acquire lands and wealth. It was not for his own sake that he desired a son. He was like a gardener of some great lord's estate. He had planted a vine, and planned to make cuttings from that vine, and so in time make for his master a vineyard of great worth. Like a good gardener, he knew that each plant needed careful attention, and proper feeding, if it was to bear

good fruit. One plant in particular he cherished, watching its growth with great delight. He knew that it would be the choicest of all the trees in his vineyard. His master would love to rest in the shade beneath it, praising its beauty and the sweetness of its fruit. If Abraham was the gardener, then the vine which he first planted was Isaac; the cuttings of that vine his descendants; the feeding of each plant the goods of this world which Abraham acquired for the sake of Isaac and his race; the most cherished tree, that tree of beauty and sweetness, was the Virgin Mary; and the Master for Whom Abraham the gardener worked, the owner of the vineyard, was God Himself, Who waited till the vineyard (the race of Isaac) was established, and then, coming, saw with content, the perfect vine in the midst of His vineyard, the Virgin Mother of God. The beauty of this tree was the perfect and sinless life of Mary; the sweetness of the fruit, the acts of her life; the shade of that tree, her virginal womb, overshadowed by the Spirit of God.

8. If Abraham then foresaw what was to be, he rejoiced in his many descendants, but most of all in that one of his descendants who, as Virgin Mother, was to bear the Son of God. This faith and holy desire Abraham handed on to Isaac, his son: your oath, he had said to the servant sent for Isaac's wife, must be sworn on the One Who is to come of my race. Isaac too handed on this same faith and desire, when he blessed his son Jacob.

9. And Jacob in blessing his twelve sons, handed on this same faith and desire in his turn to Judah. God so loved Mary, the Mother of His Son, even before the creation of

the world, and before her creating, that He gave to those He had specially chosen as His friends some foreknowledge of her, for their consolation. First to the Angels, then to Adam, and then to the Patriarchs, the creation of Mary was a thing of wonder and joy.

10. We read in the Bible of Adam's original state of happiness. Then of his disobedience to God, which brought so much suffering and sorrow. We are not told that he continued in disobedience. His sorrow was not so much the unhappiness he had brought on himself, but rather the offence he had committed against God. Created by God, owing his existence and his happiness to God, he had turned against God, and so justly deserved God's anger. This was true sorrow, bringing with it repentance and humility. And with this true sorrow came also consolation from God. One thing, and one thing only, could have fully consoled him, the promise that God Himself should come as man, of Adam's own race, and by love and humility redeem that race which his pride had deprived of life.

GLORY BE TO THE FATHER   Glory be to the Father, and to the Son, and to the Holy Spirit, as it was in the beginning, is now and ever shall be, world without end. Amen.

THE FATIMA PRAYER   O my Jesus, forgive us our sins, save us from the fires of hell, lead all souls to heaven, especially those in most need of Thy mercy.

The Birth of the Immaculate Virgin Mary to Sts. Joachim and Anne

THE FRUIT OF THIS MYSTERY

Love of Holy Purity

THE JUSTICE OF GOD flashed forth when He drove Adam from the garden of Paradise for tasting the forbidden fruit of the tree of knowledge. The mercy of God entered sweetly into this world when the Virgin Mary was born, whom we may fittingly name the Tree of Life. The justice of God drove out Adam and Eve into instant exile and misery, for their disobeying. The mercy of God gently invites and attracts to the glory of heaven, all who seek life in obeying. Mary, the Tree of Life, grew up in this world, to the joy of the Angels in heaven. They longed for the fruit of this tree, which was Christ, and they rejoiced that the great love of God would be made known among men, and that the heavenly ranks would increase in number.

OUR FATHER   Our Father, Who art in Heaven, hallowed be Thy name, Thy kingdom come, Thy will be done, on earth as it is in heaven. Give us this day our daily bread; and forgive us our trespasses, as we forgive those who trespass against us; and lead us not into temptation, but deliver us from evil. Amen.

HAIL MARY (10)   Hail Mary, Full of Grace, the Lord is with thee. Blessed art thou among women and blessed is the fruit of thy womb, Jesus. Holy Mary, Mother of God, pray for us sinners now, and at the hour of our death. Amen.

1. May you be blessed and revered, my Lady, O Virgin Mary, most holy Mother of God. You are, in truth, His best creation; and no one has ever loved Him so intimately as you, O glorious Lady. May you be praised, my Lady, O Virgin Mary, Mother of God. That same angel by whom Christ was announced to you announced you yourself to your own father and mother; and of their honest wedlock you were conceived and begotten.

2. The union of man and woman in a holy marriage was most pleasing to God, for He willed to choose the child

of such a union as the Mother of Christ. The eagle, flying above the earth, looks down at the trees, and choosing with its sharp eyes the tallest tree, one firmly rooted to withstand the storms, one that cannot be climbed, one that nothing can fall on, builds there its next, God sees, with penetrating gaze, all things, both present and future. He looked therefore among all men and women, from the beginning to the end of time, for a husband and wife fit for the bearing of the child of His choice. He found none so worthy as Joachim and Anne, who lived together in holiness and a love for each other born of their love for Him. It was to them He entrusted the one who was to be mother of His son. She was to be, as it were, the eagle's nest, in which He could find protection and shelter. Joachim and Anne were the tall tree in which this nest would be built, firmly rooted in a union based on the love and honour of God; the branches of this tree their lifelong thought for the will of God, and their desire for a child, not for their own sake, but to beget one who would grow to love God and serve Him as they themselves did.

3. The tallness of this tree, beyond the reach of the winds, and higher than all around, was the height of holiness which Joachim and Anne had attained, beyond the attacks of Satan, untroubled, except by the thought that God's honour was many times assailed by the sins of many, with no thought of honour or worldly possessions, no pride or ambition to move them from their selfless love of God. God knew that for the birth of the Mother of Christ, none holier could be found than Joachim and Anne. What a treasure you held, blessed Anne, while she who was to be Mother of God rested in your womb. How precious to God that seed of Mary's life

in your womb, more precious than the offspring of all men on earth. Anne became God's treasure-house, keeping safe this most precious thing, this seed of so precious a life. God saw it and watched over it, for as His son was to say, where one's treasure is, there is one's heart. The Angels looked on this treasure with joy, knowing how precious it was to God their Creator. It was a holy and blessed day, to be honoured by all, the day when this precious seed was first sown. God Himself and the Angels greeted that day with great rejoicing.

4. That seed of life was ready, and at God's chosen moment, life began as He infused into it a living soul. We see the bees in summer, busy making flowers for honey; led by instinct to their sweetness, they seem often to wait for the buds to open. God foresaw, as He foresees all things, the birth of Mary, and He waited with joy as she lay hidden in her mother's womb, for He knew that none ever of those to be born would equal her in holiness. None would so make known to men His infinite love. The infusing of Mary's soul in the womb of Blessed Anne was more beautiful than the dawn of the most beautiful day. As we so often long for the dawn, so Angels and men longed for her birth. Where the nights are short in summer, so that there is little darkness, people do not notice the dawn; they wait for the sun itself, thinking of their crops and their fruits. Where the nights are quite long, even in summer, the dawn is watched for and welcomed, not only for the coming of the sun to the fields, but because men weary of the night and the darkness.

5. The Angels in heaven did not await the coming of Mary that they might see Christ, for they were ever in the light of His

presence; they longed for her, so that the love of God might be made known in the world, so that men who loved God might be strengthened in their love, and then they, the Angels, could go out to gather them as an everlasting harvest for God. But men, living in this world of sorrow and hardship, desired the coming of Mary that they might see Christ their Saviour. They longed for her coming, that they might learn from her perfect life how man should live. The Virgin Mary is foretold as the branch which would grow from the root of the father of David, to bear a flower on which the Spirit of God would rest. In her mother's womb, how light Anne's burden!, Mary was the tender branch which would soon come forth. The flower that branch would bear was Christ. He Himself, from the moment of her assent to God's message, was a richer and infinitely sweeter nourishment than blessed Anne had given to her. Though Mary was to Him the food of life, giving her own flesh and blood to be His, that He might appear in true humanity, He was to Mary her heavenly food, that she might bear Him as her child, though He was truly the Son of God.

6. The Blessed Mother said, "The Lord God united my father and mother in a marriage so chaste that there could not be found a more chaste marriage at that time. They never wanted to come together except in accordance with the Law, and only then with the intention to bring forth offspring. When an angel revealed to them that they would give birth to the Virgin from whom the salvation of the world would come, they would rather have died than to come together in carnal love; lust was dead in them. I assure you that when they did come together, it was because of divine love and because of the angel's message, not out of carnal desire, but

against their will and out of a holy love for God. In this way, my flesh was put together by their seed and through divine love. Then, when my body had been made and formed, God infused the created soul into it from His divinity, and the soul was immediately sanctified along with the body, and the angels guarded and served it day and night. When my soul was sanctified and joined to its body, my mother felt such great joy that it would have been impossible to describe it!"

7. "My name is Mary, as it is said in the Gospel. When the angels hear this name, they rejoice in their mind and thank God for the great mercy that He worked through me and with me and because they see my son's humanity glorified in His divinity. Those within the fire of purgatory rejoice exceedingly, just like a sick and bedridden man does if he receives a word of comfort that pleases his soul: he is suddenly overjoyed! When the good angels hear my name, they immediately move closer to the righteous for whom they are guardians, and rejoice over their progress in good deeds and virtues."

8. Noah's Ark was so built that no water could seep in, a ship whose timbers were carefully protected both inside and out. You, Mary, the Ark of God, would be so strong in God's grace, anointed and protected by His Holy Spirit, that no desire would ever enter your heart, either for your own glory or for the possession of earthly things. Such desires, we know, are as displeasing to God as the water which seeps into the keel of a ship, and collecting there becomes state and offensive. Noah took pride, as every captain of a ship takes pride, in the cleanliness and tidiness and brightness of the Ark. God rejoiced, Mary, in your virginity, for in you there would be no

sin, nor slightest stain of sin, to taint your perfection. Noah provided for himself and those with him, all that was needed to survive the days ahead. God chose you, Mary, for His son, that your body should provide for Him a perfect human body. Noah came from the Ark unchanged. But from you, Mary, the Ark of God, the Son of God came forth, clothed with that pure flesh and blood which He had taken from you. When Noah left the Ark, its purpose was served, it was empty and useless. But when Christ came forth from your womb, you were filled with every gift of the Holy Spirit, growing ever in holiness, not further now from Christ, but nearer to Him, and dearer even than before, united to Him on earth and in heaven for ever.

9. All heaven was ablaze with these flames of God's love, to the delight of the Angels. Yet all heaven must wait; must wait for the coming of Mary. The redemption of man, willed and foreseen by God, could not take place without her. A flame of divine love was to be kindled in Mary which would rise up to God and return so filled with His love that no corner of this world would be left cold and in darkness. When Mary was born, she was like a new lamp, all ready to be lit; to be lit by God with a light burning like the three-fold flame of His own love. The first flame of her lover was her choice, for God's glory, to ever remain a virgin. So pleasing was this to the Father that He willed to entrust to her His beloved son, that son Who is inseparable from the Divinity of Himself and the Holy Spirit. The second flame of her love was her humility, so pleasing to the Son that He willed to take from her a true human body, and that humanity which was destined to be honoured in heaven above all things. The third flame of her

love was her obedience, which brought to her from the Holy Spirit the fullness of grace.

10. The fall of angels and of men did not lessen the power of God, nor take from His crown of glory. The wisdom of God turned their sin into an even greater glory for Himself. For your creation, Mary, gave such glory to God, that what was refused Him by angels and men was made good a thousand times over. Virgin Mary, our Queen and our hope of salvation, you may truly be called the crown of God's honour. Through you He showed His divine power. From you He won more honour and glory greater than from all other creatures. The angels knew, even before your creating, that by your holiness and humility you would overcome the pride of the Devil and his hatred for man. They had seen how man had fallen into misery, but in their contemplation of God, they still rejoiced, knowing well what great things God would do, Mary, through your lowliness, when His creating brought you to be.

GLORY BE TO THE FATHER   Glory be to the Father, and to the Son, and to the Holy Spirit, as it was in the beginning, is now and ever shall be, world without end. Amen.

THE FATIMA PRAYER   O my Jesus, forgive us our sins, save us from the fires of hell, lead all souls to heaven, especially those in most need of Thy mercy.

The Presentation of Mary in the Temple as a Girl

THE FRUIT OF THIS MYSTERY

The desire to preserve all Catholic children in their baptismal innocence

SPEAKING OF THE BEAUTY of Mary, we think of lovely things: her sacred body is like a vase of purest crystal; her soul like a lantern of clearest light; her mind like a fountain of water rising up into the air, then falling in cool streams to the deep valley. Passing from infancy to childhood, to the age when she was able to understand, she began to think of the existence of God, and how He made all things, and especially man, for His own eternal glory, and how His justice embraces all things.

OUR FATHER   Our Father, Who art in Heaven, hallowed be Thy name, Thy kingdom come, Thy will be done, on earth as it is in heaven. Give us this day our daily bread; and forgive us our trespasses, as we forgive those who trespass against us; and lead us not into temptation, but deliver us from evil. Amen.

HAIL MARY (10)   Hail Mary, Full of Grace, the Lord is with thee. Blessed art thou among women and blessed is the fruit of thy womb, Jesus. Holy Mary, Mother of God, pray for us sinners now, and at the hour of our death. Amen.

1. We may believe too that Mary developed in understanding earlier than others. Since the coming of Mary was such joy to God and the Angels, men too must rejoice, and give glory and honour to God, Who chose her from all His creation by eternal decree and willed that she should be born among sinners, to bring forth in sinlessness the Saviour of the World.

2. It is true that the flames of Mary's love were not lit within her at the moment of her birth. She was still, as other children, only a little one, unaware of God's will. Yet God took more pleasure in her than in all other beings. She was like a sweet-sounding harp, not yet in tune; but He Whose treasure she was knew how lovely the music He would make with her.

3. May you be blessed, my Lady, O Virgin Mary. In your most holy infancy, immediately after your weaning, you were borne by your parents to the temple of God and were, with other virgins, entrusted to the keeping of the devout high priest.

4. May you be praised my Lady, O Virgin Mary. When you reached that age at which you understood that God was your Creator, you immediately began to love Him intimately above all things. Then too you most discreetly ordered your time, both day and night, by means of various offices and exercises in honour of God. Your sleep, too, and the food for your glorious body were so temperately regulated by you that you were always fit for God's service.

5. Her thoughts reached out to God, as the waters of the fountain rise into the air; then, like those waters flowing down to the valley her thoughts returned to herself and brought her a most profound humility. The Church sings of Christ leaving and returning to the Father, though He was ever with the Father and the Father ever with Him. Mary's thoughts reached up to heaven in contemplation and grasped God by faith. Then in the love with which God possessed her, she turned her mind again to God and to herself, never losing her thought of God. Together with hope and trust, and with holy fear, the fire of this love inflamed her heart, as the flame in the brightest of lanterns.

6. How soon she learnt to appreciate God's love, and treasure it with all her being! She understood the perfect subjection that was required of body to soul, and no discord ever troubled her, so that in body she was purer than purest crystal.

Think of this love as a lily which God had planted, bearing flowers of great beauty. This lily was rooted in Our Lady's most powerful virtues. The flowers of her good works adorned her soul and gave great joy to God and His Angels.

7. With such beauty of soul, Mary surpassed all other created things. God willed that only through her should His promise be fulfilled. Her love left no blemish or defect, not even the smallest. In nothing could the enemy claim victory over her. If then she was so pleasing in the sight of God and the Angels, may we not think that she had also great earthly beauty? Those who saw her looked with delight, and knew that her loveliness was born of her love for God. They saw her, and loved to see her, and were led to a new love for God. They watched her, and loved to be with her, and knew that no evil could touch them, nothing sinful attract them, in the presence of her beauty and holiness.

8. With our slow and clouded minds, it is hard for us to appreciate that moment when Mary first knew God and gave herself to Him. His will became her one desire and her joy. She saw how she owed everything to His creating; but she knew that according to His plan, her will was free, to choose or refuse His will and His way. She saw the blessings which God had already bestowed, and for these alone she chose to love Him in return, and to love Him for ever.

9. The holy maiden learnt that He Who created all would not rest content, but would Himself come to His creation as redeemer of His creatures. And this out of love alone. She learnt that man's will, free to choose good or evil, could make

satisfaction to God through love, or incur His anger by sin. Mary was like a captain of a ship. The captain of a ship knows what dangers lie ahead, and he charts his voyage to avoid the storms. He watches the ship's course, and works out the distance sailed, and the distance still to sail before arriving in port. Every rope, every piece of equipment is in place and ready for use. The cargo he carries must reach port as quickly as possible. Every detail of the voyage must be worked out ahead. From the earliest moment of her understanding, Our Lady chose once for all the entire course of her life.

10. O my Lady, O Virgin Mary, may your tongue be praised, so pleasing to God and to the angels. You never harmed anyone through the words uttered by your tongue, but rather, they always came forth to someone's advantage. Your words were very prudent, and all found them sweeter to hear than the sweetest fruit is sweet to taste. O my Queen and my Lady, O Virgin Mary, may your blessed mouth and your lips be praised above the loveliness of roses and all other flowers, and especially for your blessed and humble word in which you responded to God's angel. By virtue of that word, you diminished the power of the demons in hell and honourably restored the choirs of angels in heaven.

GLORY BE TO THE FATHER   Glory be to the Father, and to the Son, and to the Holy Spirit, as it was in the beginning, is now and ever shall be, world without end. Amen.

THE FATIMA PRAYER   O my Jesus, forgive us our sins, save us from the fires of hell, lead all souls to heaven, especially those in most need of Thy mercy.

The Chaste Espousals
of Mary and Joseph

THE FRUIT OF THIS MYSTERY

Admiration of St. Joseph, the chaste spouse of Our Lady

AY YOU RECEIVE INFINITE glory, my Lady, O Virgin Mary, you humbly vowed your virginity to God Himself and therefore had no concern about who would betroth you, for you knew that He to Whom you had first given your faith was mightier and better than all others combined. May you be blessed, my Lady, O Virgin Mary, ablaze with ardent love for God, you lifted up all your mind and all the strength of your powers in contemplation of the Most High God to Whom you had offered your virginity. You always professed yourself most humbly as God's handmaid; and the Holy Spirit wonderfully filled you with all power and virtue.

OUR FATHER   Our Father, Who art in Heaven, hallowed be Thy name, Thy kingdom come, Thy will be done, on earth as it is in heaven. Give us this day our daily bread; and forgive us our trespasses, as we forgive those who trespass against us; and lead us not into temptation, but deliver us from evil. Amen.

HAIL MARY (10)   Hail Mary, Full of Grace, the Lord is with thee. Blessed art thou among women and blessed is the fruit of thy womb, Jesus. Holy Mary, Mother of God, pray for us sinners now, and at the hour of our death. Amen.

1. As soon as she had understood God's will, the Blessed Virgin set her course according to His commandments. She was watchful at all times that her attention should never be distracted from God. She took care, when those around her spoke of their ambitions, their successes or failures, not to let herself become less devout in her service of God. Anything contrary to God's law she knew at once as a danger to be avoided at all cost.

2. With this self-training and discipline, all that she did was good. All that she said, all that she listened to, all that she gave her attention to, was sensible and wise. Her work was

useful to herself and to others, and each journey she made had some good reason. The trials of life she accepted with patience and joy. Her one thought was God. Her one desire was to be forever with Him, to offer to Him all her love and her praise in return for all He had done for her. She won so perfect a life from God, Who is the giver of all good things, the highest holiness and glory. It is no wonder that God lover her more than all other creatures.

3. O my Lady, O Virgin Mary, may your forehead and your most honest face be together praised above the whiteness of the moon, for none of the faithful in this dark world ever looked to you without feeling some spiritual consolation poured into himself at the sight of you. May you be blessed, my Lady, O Virgin Mary, your eyebrows and your eyelids exceed in the brightness of their splendour the rays of the sun. May your most chaste eyes be blessed, O my Lady, O Virgin Mary, they coveted none of the transitory things that they saw in this world. As often as you lifted up your eyes, their appearance excelled the splendour of the stars in the sight of the whole heavenly court.

4. The Blessed Virgin said, "Although in my body I have been raised on high above all things created, I am still before God as little as when I was betrothed to Joseph. Moreover, you ought to know for very certain that before Joseph betrothed me, he understood, in the Holy Spirit, that I had vowed my virginity to God and that I was immaculate in thought, word, and deed. He betrothed me with the intention that he might serve me, treating me as his lady, not as his wife.

5. "Therefore, just as I was humble in the world, known to God alone and to Joseph, so too am I humble now as I sit on a most sublime throne, ready to present to God the rational prayers of all. But some I answer by means of divine outpourings. To others, however, I speak more secretly as is pleasing to God."

6. O my Lady, O Virgin Mary, may your most honest ears be honoured above all the forces of the sea and above the motion of all the waters; for your ears ever manfully militated against all the unclean flux of worldly hearing. O Virgin Mary, my Mistress, may your most sweet nose be revered! By the power of the Holy Spirit, it never drew or sent forth a breath without all your thought being ever in the presence of the Most High. Although at times you slept, you never turned your will from Him. Therefore, to that same nose of yours be ever given an odour of sweetness, praise, and honour above the mingled odour of all spices and fragrances of this world.

7. The Lord explained, "O friend, I preferred to be born of a virgin because that which is purest befits Me Who am God most pure. Whilst the act of carnal union was established by divine commandment in order that nature might bear its fruits, it brings greater glory to act above and beyond the commandment. For it is more virtuous and generous to be in the fire of tribulation and not to burn than to be without fire and still want to be crowned. Now, since virginity is like the fairest path to heaven while marriage is more like a road, it befitted Me, God most pure, to rest in a virgin most pure. Just as the first man was created from the virgin earth, not yet polluted by blood, and because Adam and Eve committed

their sin while they were still in a sound state of nature, so too I, God, wished to be received in the purest vessel so as to transform everything by My goodness."

8. Our Lord said, "I intimated all the mysteries of my incarnation to the prophets, so that these mysteries might the more firmly be believed the longer ago they had been foretold. To prove that My mother was truly a virgin before and after childbirth, Joseph's testimony was sufficient, inasmuch as he was the guardian and witness of her virginity. Some people do not believe that a virgin could conceive by divine power, because they do not realise that it is easier for Me, God, to do this than for the sun to penetrate glass. And, of course, divine justice kept the mystery of God's incarnation hidden from the devil and from men to be revealed in the time of grace."

9. O my Lady, O joy of my heart, O Virgin Mary, may your most venerable heart be glorified and revered. It was so afire for the honour of God, more so than all other creatures of heaven and earth, that the flame of its charity ascended the heights of heaven to God the Father, and, because of this, God's Son descended from the Father into your glorious womb with the fervour of the Holy Spirit. O my Lady, most fertile Virgin Mary, may your most blessed womb be blessed above all fruitfully sprouting fields. Just as the seed that has fallen upon good ground brings forth for its owner fruit a hundredfold, even so your womb, brought forth for God the Father blessed fruit, more than a thousandfold. Just as the lord of a field glories in its fertile abundance of fruit and just as the little birds and the animals feed in it with delight, even so did the blessed and fertile fruit of the little field of

your womb cause high honour for God in heaven, rejoicing for the angels, and, for humans on earth, a lavish flow of sustenance and life.

10. The Virgin Mary, alone of all men and women, was ever sinless and immune from sin. How near she was to heaven even before that very moment when the Angel Gabriel greeted her, "Hail, Full of Grace!" Indeed how pure, how holy she was, so much so that the Father entrusted to her His only Son, and the Son of the Father become the Son of Mary.

GLORY BE TO THE FATHER   Glory be to the Father, and to the Son, and to the Holy Spirit, as it was in the beginning, is now and ever shall be, world without end. Amen.

THE FATIMA PRAYER   O my Jesus, forgive us our sins, save us from the fires of hell, lead all souls to heaven, especially those in most need of Thy mercy.

CONCLUDING PRAYERS   *Upon completing the recitation of the Holy Rosary, the following prayers are customary, but others too may be added according to one's devotion and preference.*

HAIL HOLY QUEEN   Hail Holy Queen, Mother of Mercy, hail our life, our sweetness and our hope. To thee do we cry, poor banished children of Eve, to thee do we send up our sighs, mourning and weeping in this vale of tears. Turn then, most gracious advocate, thine eyes of mercy towards us, and after this, our exile, show unto us the blessed fruit of thy womb, Jesus. O clement, O loving, O sweet Virgin Mary. Pray for us O holy Mother of God, that we may be made worthy of the promises of Christ.

Let Us Pray   O God, Whose only begotten son, by His life, death and resurrection, has purchased for us the rewards of eternal life, grant we beseech Thee, that meditating on these mysteries of the most Holy Rosary of the Blessed Virgin Mary, we may both imitate what they contain and obtain what they promise, through the same Christ our Lord. Amen.

PRAYER TO SAINT MICHAEL THE ARCHANGEL   Holy Michael, the Archangel, defend us in the day of battle. Be our safeguard against the wickedness and snares of the devil. May God rebuke him, we humbly pray; and do thou, O Prince of the heavenly hosts, by the power of God thrust down into hell Satan and all the evil spirits who wander through the world seeking the ruin of souls. Amen.

MEMORARE   Remember, O most gracious Virgin Mary, that never was it known that anyone who fled to thy protection, implored thy help, or sought thine intercession was left unaided. Inspired by this confidence, I fly unto thee, O Virgin of virgins, my mother; to thee do I come, before thee I stand, sinful and sorrowful. O Mother of the Word Incarnate, despise not my petitions, but in thy mercy hear and answer me. Amen.

May the Divine Assistance remain always with us, and may the souls of the faithful departed, through the mercy of God rest in peace. Amen.

The Fifteen Daily Prayers of Saint Bridget of Sweden

For pious daily recitation for an entire leap year, or 366 days, in honour of the number wounds received by Our Blessed Lord during the time of His passion.

Recite an Our Father and Hail Mary for each Prayer.

FIRST PRAYER   O Jesus Christ! Eternal Sweetness to those who love Thee, joy surpassing all joy and all desire, Salvation and Hope of all sinners, Who hast proved that Thou hast no greater desire than to be among men, even assuming human nature at the fullness of time for the love of men, recall all the sufferings Thou hast endured from the instant of Thy conception, and especially during Thy Passion, as it was decreed and ordained from all eternity in the Divine plan.

Remember, O Lord, that during the Last Supper with Thy disciples, having washed their feet, Thou gavest them Thy Most Precious Body and Blood, and while at the same time Thou didst sweetly console them, Thou didst foretell them Thy coming Passion.

Remember the sadness and bitterness which Thou didst experience in Thy Soul as Thou Thyself bore witness saying: "My Soul is sorrowful even unto death."

Remember all the fear, anguish and pain that Thou didst suffer in Thy delicate Body before the torment of the crucifixion, when, after having prayed three times, bathed in a sweat of blood, Thou wast betrayed by Judas, Thy disciple, arrested by the people of a nation Thou hadst chosen and elevated, accused by false witnesses, unjustly judged by three judges during the flower of Thy youth and during the solemn Paschal season.

Remember that Thou wast despoiled of Thy garments and clothed in those of derision; that Thy Face and Eyes were veiled, that Thou wast buffeted, crowned with thorns, a reed placed in Thy Hands, that Thou was crushed with blows and overwhelmed with affronts and outrages.

In memory of all these pains and sufferings which Thou didst endure before Thy Passion on the Cross, grant me before my death true contrition, a sincere and entire confession, worthy satisfaction and the remission of all my sins. Amen.

SECOND PRAYER   O Jesus! True liberty of angels, Paradise of delights, remember the horror and sadness which Thou didst endure when Thy enemies, like furious lions, surrounded

Thee, and by thousands of insults, spits, blows, lacerations and other unheard-of-cruelties, tormented Thee at will. In consideration of these torments and insulting words, I beseech Thee, O my Saviour, to deliver me from all my enemies, visible and invisible, and to bring me, under Thy protection, to the perfection of eternal salvation. Amen.

THIRD PRAYER   O Jesus! Creator of Heaven and earth whom nothing can encompass or limit, Thou Who dost enfold and hold all under Thy Loving power, remember the very bitter pain Thou didst suffer when the Jews nailed Thy Sacred Hands and Feet to the Cross by blow after blow with big blunt nails, and not finding Thee in a pitiable enough state to satisfy their rage, they enlarged Thy Wounds, and added pain to pain, and with indescribable cruelty stretched Thy Body on the Cross, pulled Thee from all sides, thus dislocating Thy Limbs.

I beg of Thee, O Jesus, by the memory of this most Loving suffering of the Cross, to grant me the grace to fear Thee and to Love Thee. Amen.

FORTH PRAYER   O Jesus! Heavenly Physician, raised aloft on the Cross to heal our wounds with Thine, remember the bruises which Thou didst suffer and the weakness of all Thy Members which were distended to such a degree that never was there pain like unto Thine. From the crown of Thy Head to the Soles of Thy Feet there was not one spot on Thy Body that was not in torment, and yet, forgetting all Thy sufferings, Thou didst not cease to pray to Thy Heavenly Father for Thy enemies, saying: "Father forgive them for they know not what they do."

Through this great Mercy, and in memory of this suffering, grant that the remembrance of Thy Most Bitter Passion may effect in us a perfect contrition and the remission of all our sins. Amen.

FIFTH PRAYER   O Jesus! Mirror of eternal splendour, remember the sadness which Thou experienced, when contemplating in the light of Thy Divinity the predestination of those who would be saved by the merits of Thy Sacred Passion, Thou didst see at the same time, the great multitude of reprobates who would be damned for their sins, and Thou didst complain bitterly of those hopeless lost and unfortunate sinners. Through the abyss of compassion and pity, and especially through the goodness which Thou displayed to the good thief when Thou saidst to him: "This day, thou shalt be with Me in Paradise."

I beg of Thee, O Sweet Jesus, that at the hour of my death, Thou wilt show me mercy. Amen.

SIXTH PRAYER   O Jesus! Beloved and most desirable King, remember the grief Thou didst suffer, when naked and like a common criminal, Thou was fastened and raised on the Cross, when all Thy relatives and friends abandoned Thee, except Thy Beloved Mother, who remained close to Thee during Thy agony and whom Thou didst entrust to Thy faithful disciple when Thou saidst to Mary: "Woman, behold thy son!" and to Saint John: "Son, behold thy Mother!"

I beg of Thee O my Saviour, by the sword of sorrow which pierced the soul of Thy holy Mother, to have compassion on me in all my affliction and tribulations, both corporal and spiritual, and to assist me in all my trials, and especially at the hour of my death. Amen.

SEVENTH PRAYER   O Jesus! Inexhaustible Fountain of compassion, Who by a profound gesture of Love, said from the Cross: "I thirst!" suffered from the thirst for the salvation of the human race. I beg of Thee O my Saviour, to inflame in our hearts the desire to tend toward perfection in all our acts; and to extinguish in us the concupiscence of the flesh and the ardour of worldly desires. Amen.

EIGHTH PRAYER   O Jesus! Sweetness of hearts, delight of the spirit, by the bitterness of the vinegar and gall which Thou didst taste on the Cross for Love of us, grant us the grace to receive worthily Thy Precious Body and Blood during our life and at the hour of our death, that they may serve as a remedy and consolation for our souls. Amen.

NINTH PRAYER   O Jesus! Royal virtue, joy of the mind, recall the pain Thou didst endure when plunged in an ocean of bitterness at the approach of death, insulted, outraged by the Jews, Thou didst cry out in a loud voice that Thou was abandoned by Thy Father, saying: "My God, My God, why hast Thou forsaken me?"

Through this anguish, I beg of Thee, O my Saviour, not to abandon me in the terrors and pains of my death. Amen.

TENTH PRAYER   O Jesus! Who art the beginning and end of all things, life and virtue, remember that for our sakes Thou was plunged in an abyss of suffering from the soles of Thy Feet to the crown of Thy Head. In consideration of the enormity of Thy Wounds, teach me to keep, through pure love, Thy Commandments, whose way is wide and easy for those who love Thee. Amen.

ELEVENTH PRAYER   O Jesus! Deep abyss of mercy, I beg of Thee, in memory of Thy Wounds which penetrated to the very marrow of Thy Bones and to the depth of Thy Being, to draw me, a miserable sinner, overwhelmed by my offences, away from sin and to hide me from Thy Face justly irritated against me, hide me in Thy Wounds, until Thy anger and just indignation shall have passed away. Amen.

TWELFTH PRAYER   O Jesus! Mirror of Truth, symbol of unity, link of Charity, remember the multitude of wounds with which Thou was covered from head to foot, torn and reddened by the spilling of Thy adorable Blood. O Great and Universal Pain which Thou didst suffer in Thy virginal Flesh for Love of us! Sweetest Jesus! What is there that Thou couldst have done for us which Thou hast not done! May the fruit of Thy sufferings be renewed in my soul by the faithful remembrance of Thy Passion, and may Thy Love increase in my heart each day, until I see Thee in eternity, Thou Who art the treasury of every real good and every joy, which I beg Thee to grant me, O Sweetest Jesus, in Heaven. Amen.

THIRTEENTH PRAYER   O Jesus! Strong Lion, Immortal and Invincible King, remember the pain which Thou didst endure when all Thy strength, both moral and physical, was entirely exhausted, Thou didst bow Thy Head, saying: "It is consummated!"

Through this anguish and grief, I beg of Thee Lord Jesus,

to have mercy on me at the hour of my death when my mind will be greatly troubled and my soul will be in anguish. Amen.

FOURTEENTH PRAYER   O Jesus! Only Son of the Father, Splendour and figure of His Substance, remember the simple and humble recommendation Thou didst make of Thy Soul to Thy Eternal Father, saying: "Father, into Thy Hands I commend My Spirit!" And with Thy Body all torn, and Thy Heart Broken, and the bowels of Thy Mercy open to redeem us, Thou didst Expire. By this Precious Death, I beg of Thee O King of Saints, comfort me and help me to resist the devil, the flesh and the world, so that being dead to the world I may live for Thee alone.

I beg of Thee at the hour of my death to receive me, a pilgrim and an exile returning to Thee. Amen.

FIFTEENTH PRAYER   O Jesus! True and fruitful Vine! Remember the abundant outpouring of Blood which Thou didst so generously shed from Thy Sacred Body as juice from grapes in a wine press.

From Thy Side, pierced with a lance by a soldier, blood and water issued forth until there was not left in Thy Body a single drop, and finally, like a bundle of myrrh lifted to the top of the Cross Thy delicate Flesh was destroyed, the very Substance of Thy Body withered, and the Marrow of Thy Bones dried up.

Through this bitter Passion and through the outpouring of Thy Precious Blood, I beg of Thee, O Sweet Jesus, to receive my soul when I am in my death agony. Amen.

CONCLUSION   O Sweet Jesus! Pierce my heart so that my tears of penitence and love will be my bread day and night; may I be converted entirely to Thee, may my heart be Thy perpetual habitation, may my conversation be pleasing to Thee, and may the end of my life be so praiseworthy that I may merit Heaven and there with Thy saints, praise Thee forever. Amen.

Printed in Great Britain
by Amazon